OWN
YOUR
CAREER

No One Else Will

Published by Mission Point Press
2554 Chandler Road
Traverse City, Michigan 49696
(231) 421-9513
MissionPointPress.com

ISBN: 978-1-965278-13-0 (hardcover)
ISBN: 978-1-965278-12-3 (softcover)
Library of Congress Control Number: 2024921165

Printed in the United States of America

OWN
YOUR
CAREER

No One Else Will

100 Career
Tidbits

Second Edition

PAUL R. GOUDREAULT

Dedication

To my family: Katie, my wife and life partner for over 47 years; my daughter, Monet; and my son, Adrien. They all helped to make this book relevant to young and old career developers alike.

Recommendations

If you are ready to be in charge of creating a fulfilling life, read this fabulous book to learn how to be the CEO of your career. Put your feet up and grab a cup of coffee while you soak in Paul's insights on the little things that make a big difference in enjoying a successful career while living your best life.

—**Rosanna Ouellette-Pesicka,** Antea Group, chief people officer

This book is terrific! It covers everything you could wish for in sage career advice—it is perfect for yourself or even better, gift it to one of your own kids AFTER you read it!

—**Brian Butler,** WSP, USA, senior proposal manager

Paul has provided an experience-based, practical guide to career development that is thoughtful and straightforward. This is a book that I will share with young people whom I care about.

—**Steve Vanderboom,** Pace, founder and executive chairman

I've had this book on my bedside table for several weeks now and finally got the chance to read it. Wow! What great advice for those starting out in their career or starting to rethink a new one. As you're searching for unique ideas for graduating seniors or those looking to grow their careers, consider giving them a heads up with the sage advice in this little gem of a book.

—**Deborah Moazen,** marketing and communications leader

Own Your Career—No One Else Will is an excellent "how to" book for anyone wondering about their professional future or even their current condition! Written by a wise and experienced corporate professional, the advice provided is applicable to those in both private and public sectors. By using the author's own ADAPT model for career positioning, each chapter offers in-depth examples and real-life "tidbits" for the reader. Practical, engaging, and informative, the book is also a really good read.

—**Yvonne Caamal Canul,** former superintendent of Lansing School District

No matter your age or position in life, careers evolve, especially these days. Paul has a great way of calming the noise and settling you down to consider where or how you really want your career to evolve. We work for 40+ years and having balance, passion and always learning will lead to a more fulfilling work world than status quo job. This would be a great read for those just entering the job market or those searching for more at work. I'll be providing this as a gift for both my young nieces and a few colleagues "trying to find their way in the world." Highly recommended!

—**Cindi Sedberry,** environmental & regulatory director

Everyone should have this book on their shelf and take the time to revisit it on a regular basis. Whether you're a high school student trying to decide what to do after graduation, someone mid-career considering a change, or nearing retirement and trying to decide what comes next—this book offers a framework to thoughtfully evaluate what you're doing, where you want to go, and how you might get there.

—**Lisa Hartwig,** senior plan examiner

This book made a great Christmas present to each of my sons who are just starting out in their careers. Paul does an outstanding job in presenting his ADAPT model to managing one's career. His sage advice, based on his vast and diverse life experiences, is invaluable as he works through each element of the ADAPT model. It is a thoroughly enjoyable read for anyone interested in improving their career management skills, regardless of where one is in their career life cycle.

—**Rod DeMaso,** senior vice president, Insurance Industry

I received this book as a gift and wished I would have got it 6 years sooner. The ADAPT model gives you a great lens to view your career and identify where you are. With the helpful advice of Paul's tidbits you can make the most of the stage you are in and navigate your career on your terms. Overall, this book was an easy and short read. It was packed with good content and not much fluff. I will definitely read it more than once.

—**Josh Kersting,** freelance developer

I received this book as a gift from a good friend. This friend often sees things in me that I don't see in myself. This book reflects those feelings and inspires me. I have often felt defeated and overwhelmed. This book has a calming approach to keep you focused on the important parts in life. The ADAPT model is a simple and helpful tool that if you are not developing you should be. Most employers will not take care of you throughout your career and into retirement. Each of us needs to find how to be happy, financially stable, and comfortably retire on our own terms.

—**Jamie Shoemaker,** sales representative

I received this book as a gift (great content) and have since re-gifted it to my son who is pondering his career path. It has given him helpful insights and helping him develop his career road map. Thanks, Paul!

—**Eric Bergsma,** controller

This book is a quick, easy read with practical guidance. Even as a 21-year professional in my industry, this book offered up new insight into ways to further advance my career. Highly recommend it for new or veteran professionals.

—**Tina Raap,** principal sales & business development partner

Paul provides a clear and concise guide for all career levels and types. I found the investing in yourself and do it on your own terms themes refreshing and have been implementing the "tidbits" in my current career and life aspirations!

—**Chad Barnes,** vice president, Federal Programs HSE

An incredible and successful approach to own your career and own your path! I recommend this book to anyone in the market! From junior to senior level executives, a very smooth and delightful read.

—**Adriana Perez,** senior project director

Developing an advisory network to expand your career and business insights is a valuable lesson Paul shares. Paul uses real-life examples through his "tidbits," allowing readers to move beyond concept to application.

—**Todd Gift,** senior vice president, market sector leader

Contents

3 ADAPT—Develop: Begin, Challenge, and Find What Works for You 51

4   ADAPT—Apply: Continue Your Journey 85

5 ADAPT—Produce: Be the Best You Can, Now!. . . 121

6   ADAPT—Transition: Retire or Reinvent 157

This book is designed to help you visualize your CAREER.

Introduction

If you already have a great job, fantastic. However, many of us find ourselves searching for "what's next" in our careers. Maybe you feel stuck in a job or company, have been overlooked for promotions, or have found yourself unemployed or underemployed. It is time to refresh what you have learned about developing a career, take time to reassess your aspirations, and make a plan to accelerate your career.

Taking control of your career development can be intimidating, but it's also very rewarding. In this book, I will guide you in developing a career that aligns with your life plan, ignites your passion, and builds personal wealth. Are you ready for a 45-year career? Are you starting or ending a career? Regardless of your age or your career stage, you will succeed by taking ownership of your career and staying focused on your aspirations.

This book began as a helpful guide for my "20-something" kids and grew in scope to support all career developers. Developing a sustainable and meaningful career can help you live the life you want. You deserve a career that allows you to explore new cultures, challenges you, and provides you the financial freedom to retire or reinvent yourself.

In this book, I have laid out a simple career life cycle model called ADAPT. ADAPT has five stages that will guide you through your whole career. Additionally, I've included 100 Tidbits—short lessons learned—that offer quick and simple methods to reinforce key behaviors essential for a successful career. You will immediately recognize what life cycle stage you are in and be able to plan your next steps.

While I've been fortunate to have a 45-year career in the consulting industry, the path to that life wasn't always clear. My first inclination as a young adult was to become a long-haul truck driver. After enjoying hitchhiking trips through Canada, the United States, and Europe, I found a path to becoming CEO of two international consulting firms and the CEO and owner of a manufacturing company. I want to share with you the lessons I learned along the way.

This book is not an academic study. Rather, it's a practical guide for career planning. I hope the book, the ADAPT life cycle model, and the 100 Tidbits will be an easy and informative read. I am confident that you will reach your career aspirations, and I hope the lessons in this book will inspire your confidence too!

Enjoy a well-lived career and LIFE!

1   Why, What, and Who?

Why: The Motivations

Building a career these days is not easy. I believe it is much harder than when I launched mine. I have become obsessed with developing a career model that I can share with those who are early in their careers or just starting to plot theirs. As I enter what I call the "transition" phase of my career—I'll explain this in a bit—I want to share tidbits of advice that I hope will help you develop a successful career from the beginning. The book is designed to help you visualize your career, provide guideposts along the way, and support you in developing the next "chapter" in your career book. The goal is to provide an easy-to-read supplement to other information you gather about career development. You can expect the ideas that I present here have been lived and experienced by me and many of my colleagues.

There are no right or wrong answers, only ideas and practical observations that will help you avoid the usual career pitfalls. The overall goal? To make your career development fruitful and personally rewarding.

Today, the competition for jobs is higher, and the skill requirements grow continually. Technology, connectivity, and the global nature of business have created a workplace that demands more and more. It is also harder to get ahead. These global changes and the responses by business and society will only accelerate. The company, industry, or organization where you start your career will look very different when your career concludes.

I come from the first generation of career builders who were unlikely to remain in the same company or job for a lifetime. My generation is also one of the last that could rely on manufacturing industries for a career. When I was entering college, many of my high-school friends were getting jobs at GM, Ford, and Chrysler for salaries I would not see for 10 years. Of course, there are still manufacturing jobs, but the accelerated advancement of artificial intelligence and automation will continue to shift our workforce to more services with less of a need for manufacturing manpower. These changes are important to recognize, regardless of your career path or career stage.

My generation is also one of the first not to have a company pension. The notion that a company will take care of you from start to finish has vanished; you are truly on your own now. So, your ability to build a career while maintaining financial flexibility is more of a challenge today. It is not enough to do well for your company or organization; you must also do well for yourself.

I am not suggesting that money drive your career, but money is an important factor in choosing and building your career. Start early by developing a mindset of "investing in yourself." Develop habits that allow you to live within your means, and build wealth to give you financial flexibility throughout your career.

Things will continue to change, but one thing that should not is your desired career path and your motivation—the continual commitment to do better for yourself.

Develop a mindset of investing in yourself.

Building a Successful Career

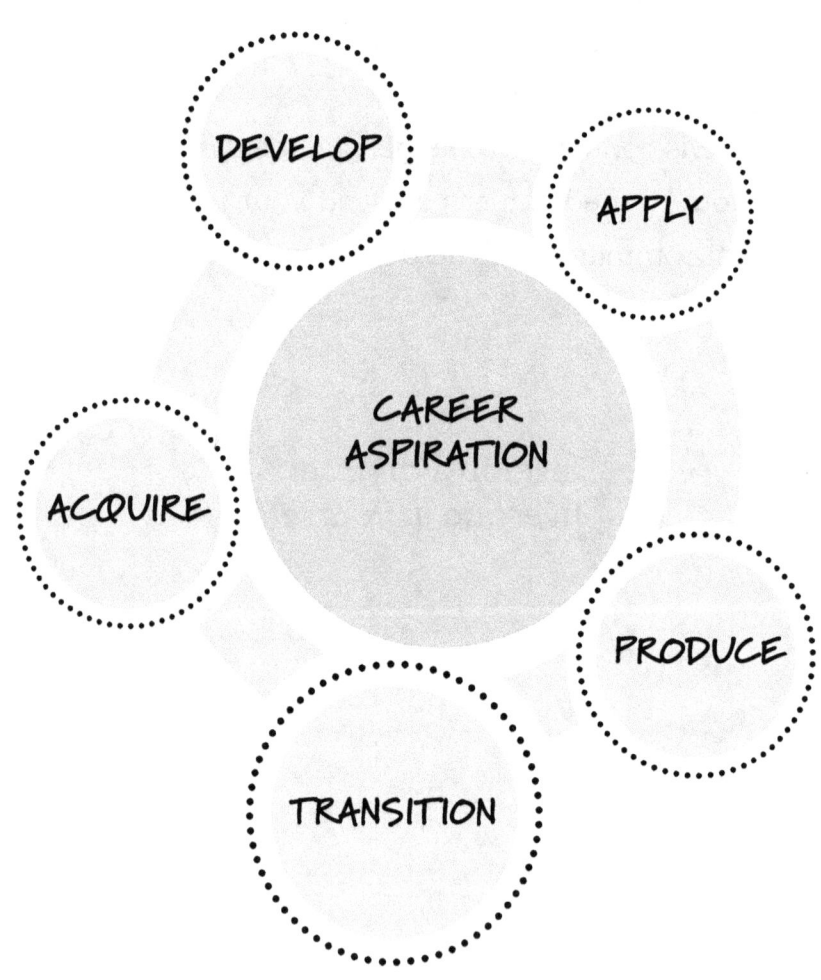

What: The ADAPT Model

The workplace is certainly more complicated these days, but it also brings great opportunities. The traditional approach to developing a career—finding a predictable career "track"—is less common. Today, you can invent your own career track. The opportunity to break out of the pack with a great idea, product, or service seems boundless. Regardless of your approach though, the ADAPT career life cycle model can help you continually navigate your career journey.

The **ADAPT (Acquire, Develop, Apply, Produce, and Transition) Model** is designed to support your career development, from start to finish. But the model also allows you to start again. That is, the model outlines a continuous process of reinvention. There are no ages, no durations, and no "must dos." No preferred career tracks. Every career is unique, with its own continuum, and requires your constant input every step along the way.

How long you are in each of the five stages—which I'll define here soon—depends on your goals and ambitions. If this model resonates with you, you should be able to quickly identify your current career stage and identify some key lessons—what I call **Tidbits**. These Tidbits can either help you become more effective in your current position, or help you move to your next career stage.

While the model's stages may look linear—meaning you must complete the first stage before moving to the next—they are not. Most of the interviews I have completed, and mentees I have coached, come back to an early career life cycle stage after redefining their career aspirations.

Fear not. The model is simple and should give you a common language to assess the challenges and opportunities ahead of you.

For example, I had a chance to talk to my electrician who was working on my house. He'd been in and out of factory and construction jobs for a number of years. But he found that he had a passion to be a professional electrician. "Life took over," he said. He is now 42 years old, working as an electrician's assistant, and is determined to get his Journey-man and Master Electrician licenses. Simply put, he redefined his career aspirations.

I also hope the model meets most of your needs. But it likely won't address them all. So be open to learning from others. Seek advice from friends, family, and colleagues you trust and respect. Don't be shy about sharing this book. It can provide an excellent reason for conversation, resulting in valuable advice and support. Most important, have some fun with it, add your own Tidbits, and feel free to modify the model to your liking. You're in the driver's seat.

Oh ... one other thing: career and life balance is also a challenge today. The crazy stereotypes of years gone by— endless hours working in the office so you can rise in the ranks—now seem ancient. It's critical that you balance a long, successful career with a rewarding life outside of work.

I don't address work and life balance much in this book. However, good career planning that achieves income and meaningful work also can create a balanced life. It starts early: by focusing on the tools necessary to successfully build a rewarding career, you will eliminate common distractions and anxieties, giving you more time to define the lifestyle you desire.

So, let's look at the FIVE STAGES.

ACQUIRE

Aquire is the first stage. This includes experimentation— brainstorming ideas on how to build the foundation of your career. It encourages you to be open-minded and to seek knowledge. It also teaches you the basic skills needed to be a contributing member of a work team or company.

Generally, this stage happens at the beginning of your career, or is used to reinvent your career. You may not have a specific career in mind, but take the time to narrow your interests, then fill those in with knowledge.

This experience is different for everyone. We all come from different backgrounds. Our family and friends will be strong influencers, and they may urge you down paths that don't fit your true passions. Don't be afraid to push back—to alter your route and expand your interests and your view of the world. You may choose formal education, apprenticeships, or the school of hard knocks.

However you proceed, you'll learn some basic things in Acquire that will set you up for future success. This stage will require investment—emotionally and financially. Don't be afraid to invest in yourself.

DEVELOP

Develop, the second stage, is when you take your skills and knowledge to the workplace. Maybe it's not your ultimate career, and likely not. However, this stage allows you to gain confidence and practice the skills you have acquired. This is a period of uncertainty, a time when you are gaining your financial independence and learning about the frustration of getting a job.

A startup job can help you continue to formulate your career and give you real-life work experience.

You also are building your collegial networks and looking for your first career break. You will be persistent, and you will be successful. You will be faced with deciding on your first job. The job may not be ideal, may not match your model of what you want to do, and will likely not pay what you expect. Don't fret; a startup job can help you continue to formulate your career and give you real-life work experience.

Start exploring the workplace, companies, institutions, or trades. You may find yourself changing jobs, roles, or industries to find the right fit for you. That's perfectly OK. You may also find that you would like to develop new skills and return to the Acquire stage. This may also be when you start to feel pressure to balance a career with your life. You are making new friends, changing cities, and becoming an independent adult. Financially, you can start to pay back some of your career investments—college loans and the like. Start small if necessary, but start now.

APPLY

The **apply** stage is taking your skills and knowledge to your preferred industry, company, or institution. You start to see a longer career window. This stage helps you test, stretch, and confirm that you are on the right path. You are learning what you do well and don't do well. Embrace your strengths and your weaknesses, because understanding both are important as you develop your career.

This is also a critical time for developing your professional network, your industry/professional knowledge, and to begin building your relationships with your customers and key stakeholders. Don't underestimate the importance of these professional relationships. They are crucial to building strong, positive relationships and will serve you well, long into the future.

This stage of your career may offer you the greatest challenge in how you manage your career pace. How fast or slow do you go in building your career? There may be a scenic route or an expressway, or something in between. Regardless of which, you can choose. Ideally, this stage will also allow you to pay off your career debt and focus on your financial future.

PRODUCE

The **produce** stage can be challenging but also the most rewarding. Here, you will need to run hard, fast, and possibly long to achieve your fullest potential. Your career has a finite duration, likely 40 to 45 years, and you should make the most of it. Hopefully in this stage you have achieved your full career potential. It's a time when you are proud of your accomplishments and have largely met your career ambitions.

You may also feel more alone than ever because you're in charge. You may be leading a team, a business, or your own company. These can be lonely roles. Ask yourself, who do you turn to for advice, how do you communicate most effectively, and what is the mark you want to make? At the risk of sounding morbid, this is when you begin to write your career eulogy.

Expectations of you in the workplace and at home can be significant. You will need to find ways to keep your batteries charged and clearly focus on the important things. Maybe most important, your judgment and behaviors will create lasting impacts on the organization and your career. Again, there are no fixed durations or ages in this model, but this is when you should commit to fully accomplishing your career ambitions. It's also a time to accumulate wealth. That sounds self-serving, but trust me, you will need wealth to build financial flexibility. So, develop and stay on a wealth-accumulation plan.

What's your career legacy going to be?

TRANSITION

Transition is the fifth stage and is a time when you transition *out* of your career, or create a new career or a new lifestyle. The most challenging part of this phase is the When? When do you begin winding down your career or take the chance to reinvent yourself? When do you choose to leave the workforce? Should you have a retirement or a startup party? A significant controlling factor will be your financial flexibility. By this time, your finances should be sound, allowing you to pursue a variety of options.

This period of your life can be very exciting, but it takes time to transition. It may be important for you to stay relevant, engaged, and interested in those things you found meaningful in your career. Or you may want to completely leave the work world and make time for yourself and family. Or you may want to start a new career. Be thoughtful and proactive about your next steps and develop a personal plan to achieve your desired outcomes.

Whatever you decide,
do so on your terms.

Who: Beginning Your Journey

This book is designed for those starting a career or those in the workforce looking for help in improving their career. There are many books, articles, and models out there to help you assess and develop your career. So how is this one different? I provide a quick guide to help you know if you are on track ... or not. If not, it helps you identify the need for mid-course corrections.

I began this effort with a focus on career professionals in their 20s. I'd been watching my two children and their friends navigate their early career stages. As I began writing, though, I soon saw that the career life cycle model could fit anyone, at any age and at every period of their career development. There may be at least three generations who might read this book.

My background comes from corporate America, so my views are biased to for-profit, corporate environments. I am also a white, boomer male. I've been privileged, for which I'm grateful. But I hope many of the book's Tidbits will help everyone, regardless of age, gender, race, or ethnicity. I have also broadened the scope to include public institutions, nonprofits, and non-American companies.

Everyone begins their journey from different starting points.

So, everyone begins their journey from different starting points. We all come from different backgrounds, financial means, and social groups.

Although there are an infinite variety of starting points, you may find yourself starting as one of the following.

APPRENTICE

Have you worked for someone for years? Learned a skill, a trade, or have simply experimented with jobs that catch your interest? You may not have a college education, but you have a clear desire to reach your fullest career potential.

Jim, a close friend in his late 20s, has a career aspiration to own a business in the real-estate market. Ideally, he wants to build or remodel homes for sale or lease. He has committed himself to be an apprentice to learn the construction trade, to learn firsthand the real-estate market. Perfect!

Being an apprentice will teach you the skills to be successful. By definition, an apprentice works with a mentor. That mentor, especially if it's someone you respect, can help you learn skills not automatically found elsewhere. Knowing these skills will obviously contribute to your own success.

ADVENTURER

Maybe you have spent much of your life traveling the world, seeing things that most of us only dream of: trips to Thailand, Australia, climbing the Andes, or sitting on the Continental Divide overlooking America's vast prairies. The experiences you gain when traveling—about different peoples, foreign cultures—will leave lasting impressions and certainly frame your life's ambition and, possibly, your career trajectory.

As a senior in high school, I took an extended hitchhiking trip to Europe with a pal of mine. I overstayed my Christmas school break and had exceeded my number of absentee days allowed to graduate. Fortunately, my mother knew I learned more on my adventure than I would have in my senior literature class! We were able to convince the school that I could graduate. Traveling also can lead to some of your greatest learning moments, such as how to problem-solve, communicate, and negotiate.

These lessons aren't necessarily taught in school, but can be experienced when you put yourself in unfamiliar environments, with only yourself to rely on.

TRADITIONALIST

You may have spent years getting a college education, pursuing knowledge through undergraduate and post-graduate studies. Chasing knowledge can be an enjoyable or painstaking journey, but either way, it pays dividends. Academia can be one of the best ways to get current and stay current with the newest  research and technology, for example. In addition, your peers and colleagues from school can be long-lasting sources of support, guidance, and opportunity.

Academic pursuit of knowledge also can help you build discipline, focus, and a love of learning. You will carry these traits forward throughout your career—and your life. Seeking knowledge, staying current, and being open to new ideas and discoveries will serve you well in any career.

ENTREPRENEUR

Maybe you want to be the next Jeff Bezos or Mark Zuckerberg. Your ambition is to build a company, be your own boss, and work for no one. This is a great aspiration and one that you can achieve with the right idea, the right pas-sion, and unceasing commitment. Your career path will likely have many starts, stops, and detours, but you will make it. It's important to maintain the right attitude and persevere.

Being an entrepreneur will introduce you to colleagues, employees, and partners who want fulfilling careers. Helping them succeed will help you succeed. Learning some of the Tidbits might help you as well. Even if you see yourself becoming your own boss, having a career plan is always a good idea.

UNDISCOVERED

Much of the career advice I've given has been to young adults who may be "stuck" in their career development. They may have come from an unsupportive family, or they've not yet settled on their passion. They may feel they've tried everything to move their career forward, but they've gained no traction.

I interviewed a 34-year-old mentee who was in the workforce for over 10 years, but never liked her job and was always seeking a better opportunity. From her viewpoint, she was running out of time! Obviously, she has much more ahead of her, with many opportunities yet to be discovered. She is in the process of developing her career aspiration, a great place to start!

Remember, you will likely be working for more than 40 years. It's expected that your career will have its stops and starts. You have one advantage, though: you know what you do not want to do. The challenge is articulating your career ambition and making a realistic plan to achieve your goals. However, it's critical that you move beyond your past and instead define your future self.

REINVENTOR

You may have reached your career ambitions and are ready for a new challenge. You've had a successful career, found meaningful work, but now you want to move on.

Alternatively, you may have started on a career path that did not fit your professional or life goals. In any case, you want to re-start by launching a new career—one more meaningful or rewarding.

The good news is that you likely know what you liked and did not like about your previous career. This could suggest either a modest or dramatic change in your career path. The choices are varied. You could retrace some of your steps in your current line of work but look to acquire new skills. Or you could get a startup job in a new industry. Or you could start your own business.

CAREER AMBITION

A final thought in this chapter: the term "career aspiration" is used a lot in this book. But what does it mean and how do I define mine? This is more than a question of "what are you going to do when you grow up?"

First of all, your career aspiration is yours. It is unique to you and you own it. Don't rely on others to define your ambitions. It is natural to see others in their careers and think, "If only I could do as well as they are doing." Don't be tempted. You should learn from other's experiences, but be careful to craft the career aspiration that best fits you.

You also will be the only one who determines if your career ambition has been achieved. And you want to dig deep for that measure of success. For example, I feel strongly that your career ambition should not be just a title. Rarely do titles define your challenges and successes.

A colleague of mine confessed that her early ambition was to be a CEO. Indeed, she accomplished this by owning her own consulting firm. But that wasn't enough. Upon reflection, she told me that her true ambition was to be a leader in her profession, be recognized for her successes, have a meaningful impact within the not-for-profit community, and be fairly compensated for her results. Her career included numerous roles with several

How do you define your aspirations?

20

companies, and she met her aspirations, but it wasn't because of her title.

So, how do you define your aspira- **_Building your_** tions? Trying to visualize the end of **_career will be a_** your career and your desired accom- **_lifetime effort._** plishments can help. Is your ambition ultimately to own your own business? Maybe you want to make a lot of money and retire early. But this visualization isn't a one-time snapshot. It is ongoing. Yes, write your career ambition down and look at it once a year. Are you on track? If so, great. But does that ambition even still fit? Your career goal may change, and that is perfectly OK. The point is that you want to remind yourself of the journey you are on and reconfirm that you are on the right path.

Building your career on your own can be scary, but it can also be rewarding. You will own your career, craft it the way you want it, and be proud of your accomplishments when you look back. No regrets, no do-overs, just a life and a career well-lived.

**A career is your opportunity to create the life you want to LIVE.**

SUMMARY

Regardless of your starting point, building your career will be a lifetime effort. It will bring you many opportunities and many challenges. A meaningful career will provide a meaningful life—one that will take you places you have never been, introduce you to lifelong friends, and inspire you in unpredictable ways.

Again, I'm hopeful this book, the ADAPT model, and the numerous Tidbits will support you in your career development.

Let us move on and dig deeper into the model and some supporting Tidbits!

2 ADAPT—
Acquire

Experiment, and Learn How to Learn

Choosing your career is important, but it's often messy and fraught with uncertainty. Most of us don't know what we want to be "when we grow up," and that's OK. But at some point, you'll need to decide. Unfortunately, selecting your path can be tough, with a lot at stake. A career is your opportunity to create the life you want to live. After all, most of you will be in the workforce for 40 years—and maybe longer. Why not make the most of it?

No pressure, right?

You don't choose a career in a vacuum, of course. So during the Acquire stage, you need to be mindful of what's out there and what's required.

So the ability to adapt to change is a skill set you want to learn. Some folks accept change easily and look forward to new "adventures"; others resist.

The most difficult challenge facing today's workforce is the speed of change, the speed of business, and the necessity to adapt.

Sure, not all change is good. But consider the alternative. Companies and technology change because the markets for goods and services change ... continually. The market is dynamic. That's a good thing. Stagnant markets typically are a sign of little to no economic growth. Fewer job opportunities. Lower pay. Thriving markets are healthy ... typically good for all of us. Companies slow to adapt to these evolving markets will fail, their workers' careers will stagnate, and upward mobility will be deferred.

So, generally, change is not only good but very good. Essential.

My advice? Challenge yourself to embrace change, remain flexible, and accept that the work world will continue to turn faster and faster. Learn the skills now that will allow you to adapt later. Innovative companies will want you on their side.

So, what should you do? You've probably heard these words before: "Find something you like doing and you will never work a day in your life." Easy to say ... less easy to realize. Often this early stage of your career search is the toughest part.

For starters, do I need to go to college? Where? Why college? Bill Gates never finished college, and he was successful! If I go to college, what should I major in? My mother was a doctor, maybe I need to be, too?

The good news is that there is a wide variety of career paths open to you. For example, there's a strong trend today toward professional-services careers—the trades—with skilled practi-tioners in high demand. Hiring a plumber, electrician, or skilled carpenter can be almost impossible these days, depending on the location. So, this is a great time for an apprentice-based career.

On the other hand, some of these skills are being replaced by artificial intelligence, automation, robotics, and smart technology. Soon autonomous long-haul trucks, fully robotic logistics, and integrated utilities will be the norm. If you once did the work, you might even be programing your successor.

I'm hearing this much more often: "I don't need to go to college," or, "What do you get with college? My friend didn't go, and he is

So ... what about college?

making a lot of money." Again, there's the Bill Gates example. More and more of our national leaders are questioning its role as well.

I have a strong opinion about this: nonsense. If you are able, you should find a college or university that fits your needs. Why? Learning who you are, what interests you, and how you manage yourself are all extremely important. Plus, *learning how to learn*—given the never-ending changes ahead of you—will be an essential skill throughout your career.

> *If you don't believe the "follow your passion" stuff, or even if you do, it is important that you look at these Acquire years as a time to "learn how to learn."*

Take the time now to invest in yourself. Colleges have a wide array of scholarships available for the hard worker if you can't foot the bill. Learn, listen, and explore what the world offers you. This is your chance.

Assume you will experiment a lot during this time. I remember coming home one day and telling my dad I was going to be an over-the-road long-haul truck driver. I wanted to see the world. My dad, a scholar of sorts, college professor and "retired" priest, was not very impressed. Somehow, I talked him into a gap year before college, and a friend of mine and I hitchhiked across the United States and Canada. With $200 in my pocket, a tent, sleeping bag, and 60-pound backpack, we were off.

Well, you probably know the end of this story: when I returned from my adventure, I was never so happy to sign up for my college classes.

What skills do you need to build a successful career? Obviously, there are plenty of articles and research on best majors, highest-paying jobs, and the newest jobs in demand. It is important to know the trends, the needs, and the available options. However, the bottom line is: what are you interested in and passionate about? Successful careers start with ambition and determination, so pursue a course you enjoy and care about.

At this point, I would argue that there is no unique path for you and your career. There are too many things over the next 40 years that will drive, distract, and guide you. So, start with your thirst and begin filling your brain with knowledge.

Also, you need to prepare yourself for a diverse workplace, and develop an ability to be flexible, approachable, and understanding of others.

> *Regardless of your focus, be sure you develop a broad interest and background.*

As a quick analogy, you are building the foundation for a successful career and life. Foundations are rooted in solid ground, are broad-based, reinforced with competent materials, and able to support great structures. The same should be true of your Acquire years. It is important to view this career life cycle stage as a time to build your foundation. Regardless of how you build it, enjoy yourself, experiment, and absorb life's learning as much as you can.

The Acquire stage is often at the beginning of your career, but it does not have to be. As you move through your career, you are likely to redefine your career aspirations because of your earlier career experiences. Or perhaps you've reconsidered your potential within your job's industry, or the career track has altered in a way that doesn't suit you. Returning to the Acquire stage is perfectly normal in developing your lifetime career. Keep in mind, too, that this move from stage to stage can occur at any point in your career— from Develop all the way up to Transition.

There are numerous examples of successful careers that have been redeveloped or reinvented by returning to the Acquire stage. Many return for professional certifications, trade license, MBA degrees, or to develop a new career track.

My daughter is an example. After graduating with her Bachelor of Arts and completing six highly successful assignments in public health, she found she wanted to pursue a clinically focused career in health care. She made the hard decision to leave her job and her career to pursue a degree and certification in nursing. She returned from her initial Develop stage to Acquire.

ASPIRATION 1

Follow Your Passion

Before each set of Tidbits within each chapter, we'll explore your Aspirations. As mentioned, your aspirations will change throughout your career. Initially your aspirations may be quite broad and influenced by your life passion. As you develop your career, you will have the opportunity to balance your passions, with your career and your life. In this chapter, we'll focus on following your passion.

When you begin your career, you likely won't know exactly what you want to do, or be able to visualize your ultimate career goal. That's OK. It is not easy to specifically define your career aspiration, but take it step by step. As you begin acquiring skills and knowledge, you will see many opportunities—some of which you might not have anticipated. You may begin to see specifics you would like to build your career around. This is not an exact science, so challenge yourself to see

At a minimum, I would suggest you write down what your **PASSIONS** *are, what type of life you would like to live, and maybe where you would like to live.*

all your opportunities and craft a career aspiration that fits you.

Forming your career aspiration can take many forms. Some may be very concrete: "I want to be an electrical engineer working in aerospace in France." Others may be less specific: "I would like to service people to improve their health and welfare."

Again, your aspiration may change with time, so there are no wrong answers. Define those things you can define now and fill in the blanks as you develop your career.

Many of my colleagues graduated with technical degrees in chemistry, geology, or engineering. Their careers started in technical roles applying the science and engineering they learned from their undergraduate studies. Many went on to gain more education, but they quickly moved into management, consulting, or became CEOs of their own businesses. It is inevitable that where you start your career will *not* be where you will end your career. However, it is important to understand your passion and develop a career aspiration that you can cultivate and fine-tune moving forward.

OK ... on to the first set of Tidbits.

TIDBITS
food for the soul

1—Get Socially Engaged

Understanding human behavior is underrated. The workplace is full of "personalities," stretching from colleagues to clients, and many others in between. Becoming part of campus life, taking psychology or sociology, and making long-term friendships will serve you well. I don't mean the Friday night bar crawls, or the party side of Greek life. I mean serious networking with peers, frequenting coffee shops, and nurturing a diverse group of friends. Having a broad group of friends can challenge you and expose you to different ways of thinking. Also, don't pass up the chance to join professional or service clubs and associations to broaden your views and learn more about yourself and your interests.

Extend yourself beyond your comfort zone. Depending on your career, you may find yourself as a minority in your company or institution. The workforce is becoming more and more diverse, so you need to be comfortable working with colleagues from different countries and cultures. Gaining an appreciation of how people interact, think, and develop their opinions is particularly important.

2—Stay Up With Technology

I assume that in as short as a year from this book's release, some technical terms will be outdated and new technology will be available to use at work and at play. So, what to do? Get current with the newest applications, how they function, and what their future value may be in the workplace. I'm not thinking of video games and joysticks here. You are likely already using technology much better than previous generations. I remember when I was completing my thesis using Fortran and a box of computer card decks. The most challenging part of my research was to ensure my computer model ran on the campus mainframe without dropping a card. Today, I can run the same model on my laptop, from an airplane at 30,000 feet.

If you are a younger professional, you are in a great position to take up technology. You also understand the speed of change in the applications and media we use to stay informed. Embrace all you can, now! Technology will change and accelerate with time. I urge you to continue to develop your understanding and use of new technologies. Keeping ahead can offer you a competitive advantage in the workforce.

3—Appreciate Science and Mathematics

Not everyone cares to—or can—solve a differential equation or remember all the taxonomy of mammals. However, developing an appreciation of scientific reasoning and empirical methods will help your problem-solving skills in the workplace. If science and mathematics are not your passions, take a favorite class in geology, biology, chemistry, or math. In general, I think the easiest way to start a career is with a STEM focus—science, technology, engineering, and mathematics—in your Acquire years. If you are choosing a technical career path, this will be built into your studies. If you're seeking a nontechnical career path, it is quite likely you will be working with people with advanced STEM degrees.

You could argue that our technology and technical solutions need to get ahead of mankind's depletions of the earth's capacity to sustain life. As a global community, we face several

We need solutions to confront some of our biggest challenges.

challenges critical to our survival: reversing the impacts of climate change, finding ways to create sustainable energy solutions, and producing enough food to feed a multiplying population. Your help will be needed in solving these challenges. While not all these solutions come from science, or the application of scientific methods, many of them will.

4—Develop a Second Language

The world is not getting any smaller. Becoming proficient in another language gives you a better appreciation for other non-native speaking clients, colleagues, communities, and their cultures. A second language will likely give you a competitive advantage when seeking employment. As educational and career opportunities grow globally, you will likely be competing with colleagues who are already fluent in a second language. If the candidate's skills, knowledge, and attitude are similar, why not hire someone who can speak to clients, employees, and partners in their native language? When living overseas with my parents as a child, I had a great opportunity to become fluent in different languages that, in hindsight, could have helped me more effectively communicate and build relationships with colleagues and clients. One of my biggest regrets is that I did not take that opportunity.

English is commonly spoken in the global workplace. If you are a native English speaker, you are very fortunate. However, in order to truly communicate with your colleagues and clients, be able to converse in their native language. Besides English, the other most commonly spoken languages include Chinese, Hindi, Spanish, French, Arabic, Bengali, and Russian. Many of the fastest-growing markets in the world are in non-native speaking English countries. The projected growth in the Middle East, Africa, India, and China is enormous. These are excellent career opportunities. Prepare yourself now.

5—Seek Travel and Adventure

The likelihood of your career taking you to other countries is high. Today's global mobility is one of the greatest organizational challenges for companies. In many organizations, you can expect an international assignment. In others, you may need to do international travel to network with colleagues and clients. Global brands, businesses, and workforces will continue to accelerate with the development of technology and the global economy. Global development will lead to more opportunities to deliver services and products globally. It may be providing health care in Senegal, water delivery solutions in Saudi Arabia, or managing a technology center in India. The list is vast.

In my career I was fortunate enough to have worked in Europe, the Middle East, China, Southeast Asia, Latin America, the United States, and Canada. Experiencing other cultures is one of the best ways to learn patience and to feed your curiosity. Spend some time traveling, navigating new environments, and developing a new set of problem-solving skills.

If you haven't traveled much, don't be afraid to get out there and plan a trip with a friend, or go solo.

You will find a sense of accomplishment and appreciation upon your return. Get your passport and don't be afraid to use it!

6—Organize Yourself

Learn how to manage challenging schedules and conflicting priorities. This is a core workplace skill. Find a system that works for you to organize your day, determine your priorities, and focus on the important stuff first. If you are a list person, make lists. If you have everything on your computer, develop a file structure that maximizes your efficiency. Organizing yourself and your daily routine can be extremely useful in helping you become an effective and efficient team member or leader.

Early in your career, you likely will find yourself in a new role but with little direction. This can be frustrating, but it can be an advantage if you can organize yourself so that you contribute to your company's mission in a noticeable way. So be prepared to confront multiple priorities, select those that are most important, and focus your time on them.

7—Get Out of the Basement

There may be unavoidable reasons for you to live at home as a young adult. Your family dynamics, your inability to pay for a place on your own, or your commitments to your family may all be factors. Staying home while attending school, developing your skills as an apprentice, or advancing your certifications is tempting. Needless to say, saving money and having laundry facilities can be very helpful and appreciated.

I don't mean to suggest that living at home is a bad thing. However, consider what you may be missing. Living on your own, or most likely with a group of friends, can help you find who you are, what you like, and what irritates you. If you think about your career, you will likely be spending more time with your coworkers than many of your family. Although you will not be living with your work colleagues, your ability to spend time with them and manage conflict will be important to a successful career. Also, your ability to be "on your own" can be very rewarding, painful at times, but ultimately affording you life skills that will help throughout your career.

8—Get Out of Your Bubble

When interviewing under-30-year-old professionals on what they would have done differently during their Acquire stage, most all agreed they would have told themselves, "Get out of your bubble."

Explore different interests beyond those that are familiar.

What does that mean? If you are in academia, spend time in the community, at job fairs, informational interviews, or get a service job. Getting good grades are not enough. If you are not in college, take a few classes, get a certification, or volunteer at the local food pantry. The key is to take the time to introduce yourself to others and extend your knowledge of your community and the workplace.

It can be difficult to explore the opportunities around you, but try to carve out time. You will need to steal at least a few hours a week from your school or work schedule. Find the closest nonprofit organization, business, or additional coursework that can help you develop new skills.

Ask yourself this: "What am I missing? Sure, I'm busy, but if only I had time to ...?" So, fill in the blank. Creating a better appreciation of how businesses, organizations, and communities work can help you develop a clearer career ambition and focus your plan.

9—Find a Group of Advisors

We're focused on your career here. But how do you develop these other skills? One of the easiest ways is to find people, friends, or family whom you respect and can learn from. Develop a network of "advisors" early in your career. Your advisors' group will change over time, but get some practice on how to build and use your network to guide you through some of these challenges.

There are some things they just don't teach in school, including how to manage your money, your time, your career, or raise kids.

Your advisors' group doesn't need to be formal; there are no rules to the game. Just engage in conversation with your group on a routine basis. It could be as informal as chatting with your uncle at the family reunion, having coffee when you can with a close friend, or setting up meetings with a respected professor.

The best time to learn is when you are faced with a challenge or a decision that can shape your future. Taking the time to build your advisors' group will allow you to access others' experience when you need it most.

10—Develop a Unique Skill

Differentiating yourself in the workplace can be hard. You cannot predict all the requirements and experience you will need to have a successful career, but you can develop a unique skill set to differentiate yourself. That's critical in today's competitive workforce. Use your advisors or colleagues to help you understand what else you could do to add to your career toolbox.

Many of the Tidbits have and will address how you develop your skills, but consider other skills you may need to thrive in the workplace. Do you have a unique skill in public speaking? Can you build a website? Maybe you can translate seemingly complex issues to simple analogs. You may be remembered best by your unique skills and ability to do things that others cannot.

11—Don't Be Above Work

You may see school as all-encompassing. I go to class, study, and if I have time, have some fun with friends. But a job gives you great experience in serving customers, working with colleagues, and earning money to support yourself. Today, the curriculum and graduation expectations are significant. Most degreed programs require an internship or apprenticeship, often unpaid. Regardless, try framing houses, being a barista, washing dishes in the cafeteria—anything to help support your work ethic and determination.

Another tip I hear from the young adults I talk to is simply to get a job, any job.

Hiring an employee is more than finding someone with a strong resume and experience. Hiring managers are interested in your ability to communicate, work with others, and demonstrate determination. I had a hiring manager in my organization whose first question for me was, "When was your first job, what was it, and can you tell me what you learned from that job?" I asked the manager later, "Why do you always ask that question?" His answer: "I can tell if the candidate is qualified by their resume, but I can't tell if they are determined and have a strong work ethic."

12—You're Not Smart Enough

Have you ever been faced with a naysayer? I'm sure you have. If not, you will. Especially in your early career stages, and particularly in your Acquire years, you may find yourself questioning your choices after being told by someone "this isn't right for you." You should welcome some criticism along the way, but you need to make the final judgment.

Early in my career, after I was accepted to graduate school, I moved to Minneapolis with my wife and dog, and I was ready to dig into my master's degree. I was focused, had evaluated my options, and was committed to getting a master's degree to support my career goals. I needed to further my education. Upon arriving at the university, I met with the department chairman.

Don't let others overly influence your choices.

That did not go so well. After we sat down, he read my file quietly and said, "You are not smart enough for this university." Of course, that was disappointing to me, but it gave me the extra motivation I needed to be successful and prove him wrong.

13—Accept That It Won't Get Any Easier

Acquiring skills and knowledge is admittedly a lifetime effort. You should always be asking questions and learning. However, if you are early in your career or you are reinventing yourself, the Acquire years can be intense and stressful. "Isn't there a better, easier, and cheaper way of doing this? When will this be over? When will I get a job?" These are all great questions, and you have the right to wonder about your situation. But I can tell you now—it's better to stick with it, to not be impatient, because it will not get easier.

It is impossible to project all of your needs early in your career. You may learn that additional education, registrations, or certification may be needed to get that coveted job that best aligns with your career aspirations. My son, while working full time, received his MBA. It certainly wasn't easy, but it allowed him to take his next career step.

If you can, get these additional credentials as soon as you can. As you develop your career, you may be overwhelmed with work, family, and life. Do it now; it won't get any easier. Your ambition and passion will help you overcome all the hard work and sacrifice you will need to reach your aspirations.

14—Find What Motivates You

As mentioned in Aspiration #1, try to understand what truly motivates you. Everyone is different, and each of our motivations can be different. As you acquire your skills or are reinventing yourself, determine what excites you, what drives you, what gives you energy. You may be surprised by what you find.

During your career and your life, you will find periods when you are challenged by your job, your colleagues, or your family commitments. You will then need to focus anew on those core things that motivate you to be successful. Accountability, responsibility, giving, caring, or the desire to be recognized by others are all strong motivators. Of course, there are others.

Focusing on your motivations will give you the energy required to be successful, regardless of the challenges you face.

15—Remain Curious

Our curiosity tends to go away as we get older. I've always wondered why organizations are so rigid, taking years to move on any strategy, to change and adapt to new conditions. I think it is because the organization and the people in that organization have lost their curiosity.

When you lose your curiosity, you talk more and listen less, you tell and don't ask, and you stop learning. Remember when you were a kid or young adult? Curiosity was our biggest advantage, our special strength that allowed us to grow. We learned to walk, talk, drive a car, differentiate between good and bad, and live on our own. As we age, we become more knowledgeable, but also more rigid. We think we know

Don't lose your curiosity! As we age, we become too knowledgeable for our own good.

things we don't, we pretend we have already "tried that," and we are compelled to "tell it like it is." Don't fall into the trap of trying to be the smartest person in the room.

Remaining curious allows you to create, learn, and develop solutions you could not have discovered if you had been too stubborn to learn. As a leader, it invites engagement from your team and it respects the collective knowledge of the organization. I was recently coaching a CEO who was sharp, but lacked curiosity. It wasn't that he lacked curiosity of others, but he resisted learning how he could change to become a better leader and businessperson. Instead of inviting feedback, he would avoid discussions that would challenge his perspective. He would fail to see reality and insist that he already knew what needed to be done. His lack of curiosity prevented him from changing in a business that required agility.

While it is true that you need to know how to be competent and effective, a common mistake many fall for is believing that the only way to progress your career is by knowing everything. But that is impossible. Having the courage to remain curious, accept that you don't have all the answers, and ask questions will lead to greater success than stubbornly relying on your own knowledge. Engage others and be the first one to change if that is what is needed.

16—Career Is Not a Bad Word

When I talk to some young career developer, they hesitate to use the word career. In some cases, they tell me they don't want a career. "I don't have a career and don't need one. I am fine working at what I do and really don't want to work my life away for a company. I'll be a TikTok influencer and life will be good." I do understand that today there are many more opportunities to be self-employed, work for multiple companies, or start a business of your own.

Developing a career is a 40- to 45-year journey.

Developing a career is a 40- to 45-year journey. Some-times you are on the expressway; other times, you're on a scenic route or refueling. Genera-tionally, things have changed. The expectations Baby Boomers had for their careers are different from the expectations of Gen X, Millennials, or Gen Z.

You will have a career whether you like it or not— shape it to align with your life.

Think about where you are today: are you developing a career or just working? How will you feel later in life if you are still "working?" Careers are developed over time, and as with anything that develops over time, a lot can go well, and a lot can go wrong.

Your expectation of your career can be unique to you, but you will have a career whether you like it or not. You have the opportunity to define your career, so why not take ownership? You set your career aspirations and you live your journey.

A career does not need to look like anyone else's— make it meaningful to you. You should look to partner with your career to allow you to live the life you desire. Shape and grow your career so that it aligns with your life. Your career should be a friend, not a foe.

17—Invest Financially—
With Reason

Good financial habits can last you a lifetime.

The cost of education has been increasing, and it is not likely to decrease over time. The investments you make will pay off if done wisely. However, be careful not to overinvest. Some careers require apprenticeships, post-graduate education, or extensive certifications/registrations. If you are committed and have the resources, great. Many of you, though, will need to take loans to pay for these costs. So, first, be absolutely sure you are in the right program. Then take advantage of scholarships, grants, or other financial support. If you anticipate large investments and potentially large debt, be sure your career can support your investments. Invest in yourself, but don't overinvest!

This is also a good time to get advice about your financial plan.

Find someone to help you begin planning for your financial freedom. This does not need to be an expert, but someone you trust. Maybe even a family member or family friend who can teach you some money-management basics. Getting an overall understanding of the stock market, how to develop a credit history, and how to budget are all part of securing a strong financial future.

Prepare yourself for a diverse workplace, and develop an ability to be flexible, approachable, and understanding of others.

SUMMARY

The Acquire stage of your career constitutes your informative career years. If you have a well-developed career aspiration, great! Regardless, develop a broad foundation of skills that will give you the tools you need beyond the degree, certification, or licenses to develop a successful career.

Today's workforce needs people who are global minded, good problem solvers, and work well with teams. The days when only your grades and curriculum get you a job are disappearing. Travel, socialize, develop broad interests, and start to develop your career ambition.

3 ADAPT—
Develop

Begin, Challenge, and
Find What Works for You

Developing your skills takes time and it is a lifetime pursuit, but look for opportunities early to develop a range of skills. There are many types of "startup" jobs in industry, manufacturing, academia, or government. You may have a clear path, and if you do, pursue it. If not, experiment.

Of course, it matters what kind of job you land, but think of this more as an

> *I am building
> my career,
> step by step.*

opportunity to test your career ambition. Think of your career in one- to two-year periods, and look for roles that will allow you to develop those skills you see important in a lifetime career. Be prepared for that neighbor or relative to ask, "So tell me, what are you doing now?" Take away that awkward pause, and tell them what you are doing, and be excited in your response, "I am building my career, step-by-step."

After graduating from college, my wife and I worked on an Indian reservation in South Dakota. Needless to say, family gatherings were interesting as we were always asked to explain what we did, and why we chose this work. Most of them had never heard of the reservation or where it was located. Moreover, not many were very interested in learning about the experience. Of course, people were friendly, but we could tell that they did not feel it was a wise "career move." I imagine they were thinking, "After 16 years of school, you are doing what?"

Remember, this is a time to experiment with your career path. Find what you are most interested in, and what makes you feel meaningful.

You can imagine that we learned a lot about ourselves. This experience helped craft our interest and our lifetime careers. I learned skills that would follow me through my career, including public speaking, writing, and negotiating. I was a minority, one of two non-Native Americans working for the tribe. I was fired twice for no apparent reason other than being non-native. I could not communicate with my colleagues in their native language. This "startup" job was the best thing for me. I was able to develop my skills and begin to narrow my journey for my lifetime career.

As I evaluated my career ambition, it was clear that I would need to go back to school and further my education if I was going to move forward with a meaningful career. Additional education is not always the answer. Maybe your biggest challenge is gaining your independence and exploring what is important to you, and what you are passionate about. In other cases, it may be as simple as finding another job or another "startup" role with a new company. Maybe it is career oriented, or maybe it is not.

Transitioning your personal passion to your career takes time. Of course, you will continue to fine-tune your career and your career ambition throughout your career, but take time now to begin understanding your personal passions and interests. Depending on your journey, you may spend several years developing your path forward, and that is OK.

Slowly, deliberately evaluate your interests, necessary skills, and narrow your career ambition.

Seek out roles that challenge you and allow you to learn new skills. Equally important to your job is finding an industry or company that aligns with your personal passions and interests. Understanding the key elements of your career, including your job, an industry, and a compatible organization, is important.

As I talk to my colleagues, friends, and younger career developers, I often hear that "I am stuck in my job—how do I get out?" Be persistent and keep focused on the future. Revisit your career ambition, and remember, again, that your career will last 40 years or so. You have time to find your path and have a successful career.

Don't get discouraged if you feel like you are just not finding your ideal job.

ASPIRATION 2

Narrowing Your Journey

As you begin your work and feel that you are on your way, you can look at your career with a more realistic, and potentially more critical eye. Experience in the workplace will help you refine your career aspiration. Let yourself be available to numerous assignments and duties. The key in the Develop stage is to assess how your passions can be translated to a successful career. Look at your earlier career aspiration and provide more insights on what type of career you desire.

Start by capturing your desired outcomes—those accomplishments you most hope to achieve in your career.

⇨ "I think I would like my own clinic. That would allow me to develop a reputable medical practice helping as many patients as possible."

⇨ "I would like to be recognized by my peers as an industry leader."

⇨ "I want to be a millionaire by age 35."

⇨ "I feel compelled to make a significant contribution to enhancing health and advancing health equity."

These are aspirational statements, and they are meant to be on the horizon—your destination after many years of hard work.

55

⇨ "I seek to be a leader in a global company."

⇨ "The most important things are to support my family and have a meaningful and fulfilling career."

⇨ "I want to make meaningful change in the lives of people in need."

They may seem still too broad, but developing a career-aspiration statement like these can provide some tangible boundaries to your career and help direct you forward.

Last, assess your skills and knowledge. Are they enough to fulfill your aspiration? You could be met with some hard decisions during this time in your career, including, "Do I have the right experience or training?" Challenge yourself to go back to school or further your experiences before moving on.

You are in control of your career, your pace, and its direction.

TIDBITS
food for the soul

18—Managers Matter

One of the most determining factors in a successful career is to work for a person you respect and who will challenge you, recognize you, and promote you. Will you ever have the perfect manager? Likely not, unless you become your own boss, but you will quickly appreciate a manager who motivates and engages you.

As you develop your career, you will find your job satisfaction and the decisions you make will be dependent on your relationship with your manager. So, when you seek job opportunities, size up your role and the company. But also check out who will be your manager.

If you are already in your career, you will likely remember your first manager. Your first and last managers are often the most memorable. As you move through your career, learn from each of your managers. Take note of those behaviors and attributes you respond well to and those you don't. This inventory will help you in your own career by recognizing your responses to future managers. You also will likely become a better manager yourself by remembering the best of your previous managers.

If you are faced with a career opportunity where you think your manager will not motivate or promote you, take a second look. In the heat of the moment, you may say, "Oh, he's not that bad." But that's not a good sign. It's likely a bad fit.

19—Communication Matters

Effective communication between you and your clients and colleagues is important. Understand that by helping them become successful, you will, too. Learn what is important to communicate and how best to communicate key messages. Be sure to truly connect with them. Find out what makes them tick, what motivates them, and what they do outside of work. For many people this comes easily, but for others, it takes work, energy, and may force them out of their comfort zone. Little by little, you will begin to understand how your clients and colleagues think, and how to best communicate with them in order to be an effective member of the team.

Be aware that as you communicate upward in your organization, you'll need to simplify and be very direct.

Your manager and her manager do not have time to get into the details. They want recommendations supported by your analysis and judgment. Similarly, if you are communicating down the organization—asking those who report to you to act—you need to be specific about the assignment, expected outcomes, and explain their responsibilities and how they benefit.

20—Personal Brand Matters

Begin developing your personal brand. What are the first and lasting impressions you want to leave with your clients and colleagues? Your brand can change over time as you develop your career, but be sure you know your strengths, weaknesses, and how you want to present yourself. These should obviously be positive and reinforcing.

Be cautious; define a brand that is you, a brand you will reinforce with your actions. Use your brand to your advantage. Consistently present yourself in a way that is aligned with your brand. Be careful to not make your brand too common. Your brand should differentiate you positively in the organization.

Your brand is only established and strengthened by your behaviors.

While your brand is uniquely yours, you should also consider the norms or culture of the organization. Ideally, your brand and the organization's culture are aligned. If not, think about changing one of them. Know, too, that it's nearly impossible to change the culture of an organization on your own.

21—Clear Roles Matter

Sometimes you get that "startup" job and you are left on your own. Entry-level roles seldom get the attention they need from managers, and therefore you might find yourself wondering what to do and feeling insecure or anxious about the role. This is an opportunity for you to exercise some control and exhibit leadership.

Defining your role and primary assignments will help you feel better about your job and provide a meaningful contribution to your organization.

You will likely have a job description, but it usually covers all the possible needs the organization may have. So take the time to evaluate the organization, your team, and your strengths. Then meet with your manager and offer to take on assignments you feel will benefit the organization the most. I am not suggesting that you chase a new role. Instead, you should intentionally develop your existing role with focus and purpose.

This is also a great time to learn how to differentiate between short-term, medium-term, and long-term goals. Depending on the organization and its ability to project long-term needs, you will need to focus on short-term and medium-term goals. So, set yourself up with meaningful assignments that are achievable—ones where you can demonstrate success within the next three to six months.

22—Effectiveness Is Important

There are many facets of effectiveness, but I believe one of the key things to understand is how to differentiate between what's important and not in driving the desired outcomes of your job. Your ability to recognize and focus on the important things will help you have a successful career. That is, learn how to make the routine and administrative activities as efficient as possible. Working long hours—being the first one in and the last one out—should give you a clue that you may not be efficient. If you find yourself working this way, seek advice on how to streamline things. Then, as you gain control of the

Learn how to compartmentalize your work.

routine activities, give yourself time to think creatively and learn new skills.

Becoming effective will naturally come as you develop your career, but try to accelerate your effectiveness early in your career. There are numerous books and publications on how to be more effective. I have found that the first step is to align your goals and assignments with those of your manager. The second challenge is filtering unnecessary work out of your daily routine. Each morning, organize your day and stay focused on those activities that move you toward your goals.

23—Mentors Are Important

This is also an important time to develop your first mentor, someone you admire in the workforce or in your circle of friends. Look for an individual who can challenge you and teach you the "nonbook" skills you need to be successful.

Your mentor should help you develop your longer career aspirations. I find that "organizational" mentor programs are not very effective unless there is a demonstrated culture to develop leaders from within the company or firm. You need to select your mentors, make the time to engage, and ask them for help.

You should have a "lifestyle" mentor and a "career" mentor. Sometimes these attributes can be found in a single mentor, but that's rare. Find mentors who will make you think critically about your life and career. Your mentor should know you, your skills, and your behaviors. A mentor can challenge you to think bigger and more broadly, beyond your current role to potential future roles.

Work at the relationship; you will get as much as you put in.

Consider your mentors as key members of your team. I have had several mentors throughout my career, some formal and many informal. Ask your mentor to help you evaluate the career path you are on: Is it a good fit? What might you do differently to achieve your career aspiration?

24—Develop Courage

The workplace can be dangerous. Every day, you are making decisions that can affect your colleagues, your clients, or yourself. You will be under pressure to decide and act, sometimes before you are comfortable or ready to act. Trust yourself and have the courage to make the decision, but be accountable for the outcomes and learn from any poor decisions.

Teams and managers must be counted on when decisions need to be made and actions taken. I have worked with clients and organizations where teams are paralyzed by their inability to decide on a clear action plan. The organization waits while nothing happens, perpetuating the status quo. Status quo in today's workplace will eventually kill a business. Don't contribute to this indecision.

Yes, not all your decisions or actions will lead to the best results. Generally, there are many options in deciding a path forward. There is no single, unique solution that will generate the perfect results. But the saying goes, "Not to decide is to decide." That is, it's generally better to chart a path forward than to chart no path at all. The decisions that are made and the actions taken will allow you to learn how to accelerate the desired outcomes.

25—Sit in Front

Sitting in front has many advantages. First, it is likely you will become more engaged in the meeting or presentation, and so, learn more. Second, you will make your presence known! This is important. Your success depends a great deal on how others perceive you. Being thought of as interested, engaged, and curious is always good. So, you should actively listen, take notes, and ask a good question or two, if appropriate. Conversely, don't fall asleep, daydream, or have an attitude.

Try to attend company or organizational events including town halls, training sessions, or industry presentations. Take the time to introduce yourself to the presenter after the session. A simple, "Thank you, I found your presentation very informative, interesting, and exciting," is all you need to say. Be honest, of course. If the presentation was boring, hold off on the praise. A speaker will know if you're being forthright. But if the session was valuable, let the presenter know that.

How many times do you walk into a room and the "front" of the room is empty?

Remember, it is more than showing up. It's how you show up that counts. Make yourself known and demonstrate positive behaviors. Employers like to see these characteristics in their leaders.

26—Start Selling

Start developing your value proposition as a leader and a colleague. Your value to an organization and to your coworkers will change throughout your career, but take the time to think through what and how you bring value. What is your personal value proposition?

Achieving your assignments and meeting your organization's expectations is the first step. Beyond that, what future value can you bring to your organization and team? Does the organization see you as a future leader, a long-term and committed employee?

Often it is hard to sell yourself, but be sure your closest colleagues understand your commitment, your work ethic, and your ability to perform. Take time to recognize your accomplishments, congratulate your team and let your manager know you are ready for another challenge.

27—Control Only What You Can

Somewhere along your career, the complexity of your role, the culture of the organization, or the dynamics of the people you work with may feel like too much. You will see this manifest itself in numerous ways. A colleague of yours may get that promotion rather than you. Your organization may go through a major merger or reorganization. Maybe your manager moves on and the new manager is not a good fit. While these things will happen throughout your career, now is a good time to learn how to handle them.

The first order of business is to not trouble yourself with actions or decisions outside your control. This is not about ignoring issues or using the excuse "this is not in my job description." You should challenge those that you think are not right, or will not lead to the right outcomes, but pick your battles wisely. It is much more effective to focus on the positive and constructive actions that you believe will help meet your goals.

If your colleagues are discouraged or focused on negativity, don't be one of them. You may not control the decisions in the workplace, but you can always control your response and reactions as a team member.

If you need to take on an issue, be direct, be respectful, and try to discuss your concerns directly with those who can act. If this is a management issue, take it up with your manager. If this is a client issue, take it up with your client. Some of these harder conversations can lead to career-lasting respect and support from your colleagues and clients.

28—Learn How to Be a Contributing Team Member

This might be easy for some of you, not so easy for others. Why is it important? Primarily, because your career will depend on how well you work with others and lead others to perform as a team.

There are few careers where you can be a lone contributor. Instead, your solutions and results will be attributed to your team, not to you individually. Also, you may be working with many of your team members and other colleagues throughout your career. You don't want the reputation as a loner—in it just for yourself.

Your team members will want you to engage and contribute to solutions. Work hard to build respect, and likewise, you should respect others. Try not to be exclusive; instead, embrace diversity.

29—Brains, Attitude, and Luck

While you should not rely on luck alone, it can be a hidden ingredient to support your knowledge and commitment to your career. You will find that hiring and advancement decisions are determined by many things. At times, you just might be the right person. Yes, your knowledge and positive attitude are important, but many factors are out of your control. Maybe the role needs immediate attention, maybe the firm has made a commitment to hire from within, or maybe you are the easiest decision to make. Often, these things are driven by luck.

It shouldn't be surprising that luck can have a lot to do with a successful career.

Regardless of the reasons, we all welcome luck when it comes. I am a believer that luck arrives for those who deserve it. Not all agree. But the best approach is to fully develop your career plan. Then, if luck comes around, it can only accelerate your success.

So, luck alone may deliver some short-term results. That said, you need to be sure to keep your lifetime career in focus and learn not to depend on luck. At times you may think everyone else gets all the luck. But don't lose your focus because of it.

30—Don't Second Guess Your Judgment

As you begin developing your career, you will find that often there are no obvious right or wrong answers. Your ability to define challenges and offer solutions will rely more and more on your judgment. So, it's important to understand how you process information and make decisions ... the bedrocks of sound judgment.

Depending on your career, an organization can have a certain personality that drives its decisions. Some organizations are very process driven, some are more analytical, and others may be very entrepreneurial. But you also have a personality that drives your decisions.

So, it's important that you understand early in your career how you decide on things. Why? First, you'll want to examine your efficiency in decision-making; that is, evaluate the steps you take in gathering research, talking with others, and asking the right questions. Establishing a basic process will make the decision-making more thorough and also make it happen more quickly. It's a more effective use of your time. Second, self-examination forces you to understand your blind spots—finding those things that you normally do not include in your decision-making. Here, it helps to find colleagues and team members who will complement your decision-making approach.

If you accomplish the above steps, you will have fortified your ability to make the right decisions. You will have ample reason then, to trust your own judgment.

31—Don't Be Married to Your Job

Keeping a balance between the work you do and your career is important. I hope your career will be full of companies and people who support you and your ambition. You should feel that you are fairly treated for the contributions you make to your company. Assessing this on an ongoing basis is important.

Unfortunately, at times, you may feel you are giving more to the organization than you are getting. Be patient, but if you don't feel fairly treated, it may be time to move on.

Often, employees and employers develop a "psychological contract" that defines mutual expectations. The tough part is that these expectations usually aren't formally communicated. You should develop such a contract that clearly outlines your career expectations. Share this

Be open to new opportunities, whether you seek them or they are offered to you. It is your career. You must do what is best for you.

contract with your manager if appropriate, and if you think it would be constructive. If your employer is failing to meet your expectations, consider looking for new opportunities.

Leaving your job and finding another job can be intimidating. First, you may be leaving a paycheck. Second, you will be leaving a familiar network of colleagues and starting over. Regardless, you need to find an organization and a role where you feel your contributions are recognized and valued.

32—If Your Boss Is Successful, You Will Be Successful

Have you ever been working on a team where you are barely getting by? Your goals are unachievable, your colleagues are complaining and your manager does not seem to care about the success of the team? If this is the case, you and your colleagues are "guilty through association." Individually you may be performing on your assignments, but the team and the manager are failing to meet their expectations. Hopefully the organization will recognize that the goals are too ambitious or that the manager is ineffective in communicating to the team clear expectations. If the situation is too severe, maybe the manager will be replaced and there will be changes to the team. Ineffective managers blame their team for their failures.

> *Remember, you are part of something bigger. Look beyond your own success, help others be successful!*

Alternatively, have you ever been on a "World Cup Winning Team" or a "Superbowl Winning Team"? Your manager and your team have been successful! You have fulfilled the commitments the manager made to the organization. You and your team executed on your assignments and made it happen. Maybe you are one of the star performers, the team MVP or maybe just part of a winning team. Regardless you will always be associated as being successful.

Remember, you are part of something bigger. Your assignment from your manager is a portion of their assignment. Managers are in place to coordinate the efforts of a team to achieve goals that cannot be achieved individually. Good managers are successful in communicating clear expectations and providing the context for the bigger picture, the ultimate challenge. A successful manager is recognized by the organization and is given opportunities to grow in the organization. Good managers also recognize their team for their contributions. This recognition gives you opportunities to accept other more challenging assignments, be promoted into roles you have identified as beneficial to your career, or even become the manager as your successful manager gets promoted!

Look beyond your own success. Help others be successful; you will benefit from their success.

33—Pack Your Lunch

If you have been in a middle school cafeteria lately, not much has changed. The noon hour and the lunch period are where the real learning begins. Where do you sit? With the cool kids, the jocks, the smart kids, or do you randomly pick a table and have a seat? Of course, we don't eat in school cafeterias anymore, but we can choose who we "eat with."

In the workplace, it is easy to sit with the cool kids! It is also easy to sit with the same people every day. Seeking out people you know is easy; seeking out those people you don't know is more difficult. I would not encourage you to sit with the bullies or the delinquents, but expanding your relationships in the workplace is important. Challenge yourself to get to know your colleagues within your work group and outside your work group. It is a great opportunity to learn about what people do at work, what they value outside of work, and how you might connect with their common interests.

Don't always sit with the cool kids! We can choose who we eat with. Make friending fun!

As a consultant, I facilitate a lot of meetings, and I am always amazed at how people will sit in their same seats, day after day. Do you switch seats during long meetings, conferences, or training sessions? I find that the perceived leaders in the organization will attempt to change seats, and at first it is weird and a bit uncomfortable. However, over the course of the meeting, I see greater excitement and engagement at the new table. The table talk increases, people are more eager to share their ideas, and they become more creative in their solutions.

Create your own scavenger hunt. Make friending fun! Take a look around you when you are sitting at your next meeting. Make a note to yourself about what you would like to learn from one of your colleagues. Maybe it is work related, maybe not. After the meeting, or the next time you are "eating lunch," find a way to introduce yourself and learn more about them.

Don't always sit with the cool kids!

34—Keep the Cup Half Full

Remaining positive at work can sometimes be hard. If you think about it, an organization is like a small city or community. You live in an environment with certain norms or accepted behaviors and are always in a perpetual traffic jam with deadlines and deliverables. Sometimes your communication breaks down, laptops don't work, and your neighbor is always complaining about something. Sound familiar?

It is easy to get stuck in the daily hustle of work. Staying busy is a good thing, but it has its limits. Burnout doesn't necessarily come

Break through the institutional noise and clutter.

from working too many hours, but instead from setting unachievable goals, lack of support, and underperforming team members. Finding ways to break through the institutional noise and clutter is key to developing a successful career.

One of my favorite books is *Man's Search for Meaning* by Victor Frankl. The story is based on his observation as a psychologist while imprisoned in a Nazi concentration camp. In it, he asked, "Why do the strong perish and the seemingly weak survive?" One of his conclusions was that we are not always in control of our environment, but we are always in control of our response to our environment. This teaching comes in very handy when you look at how you want to "show up for work."

> *When you pour your coffee or tea, also pour yourself a glass of good intentions.*

Occasionally, you will find yourself talking to a colleague about frustrations at work, or listening to a leader preach about behaviors he himself does not practice, or getting chewed out by a client who is not satisfied with your work. These situations are inevitable, and it's up to you to determine how you respond to them. Remain positive, and both you and your colleagues will appreciate your ability to see the irony or truth in the moment. Don't be shy of voicing your opinion if you feel compelled, but find a way to be constructive and respectful.

At the end of the day, being positive is a necessary leadership trait. Furthermore, your colleagues will appreciate you more if you are pleasant. In the morning as you get your coffee or tea, also pour yourself a glass of good intentions and keep it full during the day—or at least more than half-full.

35—Keep the Ball on the Other Side of the Court

Have you ever played tennis, or the new rage, pickleball? Both are great games that involve strategy and teamwork. But the fundamental goal is to put the ball on the other side of the court. Understanding where you are going to hit the ball and hitting it to the place you intended is the name of the game. Simple, right? These two games have a lot of similarities to managing your effectiveness at work. You have a role with primary assignments. In order to execute on your assignments, you have certain required tasks. Maybe it's doing status reports, specific client deliverables, or just managing the administrivia in your organization.

The real game is to put the ball on the other side of the court.

It is all about understanding what the expectations are (knowing where you should hit the ball) and completing the task (hitting the ball). In many cases, it is up to you to formulate the tasks associated with your assignments; in other cases, the tasks are described to you. Set yourself up for success by managing your tasks to ensure they are achievable and within your control, whenever possible. If you are relying on others, be sure you have the A+ team.

As with tennis and pickleball, you only have so much time to hit the ball. Preparing to hit the ball is as important as your swing or your magic spin. You have to get to the ball, position your feet and your body, and time the swing to place the ball where you want it to go. It's the same with delivering on your assignments. Consider your team's opinions, evaluate all your possible actions, and ensure the quality of the deliverable is sufficient to meet the expectations.

But remember, the point of the game is to place the ball on the other side of the court where you intended it to go. Hit the ball and deliver your assignments on time. Now, prepare yourself for the return.

Preparing to hit the ball is as important as your swing or your magic spin.

36—Bring Commitment

Commitment means different things to different people. To me, the workplace is like a friendly game of euchre. If you haven't played euchre, it's a game of four players divided into two teams. You are paired up with a team member to win against the other team. You remain blind to the cards your team member has, but it is up to you to play off your team member's cards. In return, your team member must play off of your cards to win a hand. The team that wins the most hands in the round wins that round. It's fun—try it if you have not already.

The workplace is like a friendly game of euchre.

How does a card game resemble work? First, at work you are required to play as a team. Seldom do you know the exact capabilities and knowledge of your team members. Often you don't know them personally or what they value in your relationship or the outcome of your efforts together. Secondly, you are competing against others. In your organization, you are competing to excel at your assignments to meet the needs of the organization and those who you serve. Lastly, you need to be committed to your partner. If your partner makes a misstep, you will cover. If you make a misstep, your partner will cover.

When you come to work, come committed. The best results are achieved by those who understand the importance of the outcome and remain committed to fulfilling the expectations. If you cannot remain committed, check yourself. Commitment comes from a feeling of shared value. You remain committed when you believe the challenge is aligned with your core values and will achieve results you can be proud of. In addition, most challenges worth the fight will also benefit you either in the short term or long term.

Commitment comes from a feeling of shared value.

Commitment drives success—remain committed and achieve your desired results.

37—Goldilocks Organization

Have you ever said to yourself, "I need some help with my work assignments, and no one is here to help me?" Or maybe the contrary, "I can't get any work done around here without someone looking over my shoulder." What you are feeling, in either case, is an organization that is not structured optimally for the type of work the organization does. Like the story of Goldilocks, the

porridge is either too hot, too cold, or just right. Organizations have structures in place to manage work and deliver results. Structures are built over time and evolve with the organization, both its challenges and its opportunities. As in Goldilocks, the optimal organiza-
tions rarely exist. Organizations either have too few layers or too many. Seldom do organizations have the "just right" number of layers.

Seldom do organizations have the "just right" number of layers.

If an organization has too few layers, you find yourself on your own. In some cases, this can feel good; you have freedom and latitude on how you do your work. In other cases, you are not getting the support you need to be successful. Many startups or rapidly evolving organizations are purposely flat, with few tiers of managers. Often these organizations are nimble, but may lack the ability to sustain their success. If your organiza-
tion has too many layers, you will feel micromanaged. You are not only being told what to do, but how to do it as well. As a newer employee or professional, you may feel comfortable with this and value the coaching you are getting. Generally, organizations with

If an organization has too few layers, you find yourself on your own.

too many layers are less nimble and eventually need to change to remain relevant.

The "just right" organization is one where you are clear on your role and assignments, you understand the broader context for your assignments, and you are supported with the resources necessary to be successful. In addition, the organization has ways to measure performance. Performance is judged by doing the right things, not solely by doing things right.

> *If your organization has too many layers, you will feel micromanaged.*

So, what can you do? Understand that organizational structures are rarely optimal. Seek organizations that are compatible with your working style. Also, don't panic: organizational structures will change over time, and maybe you just need to wait it out or make the change yourself.

38—Financial Payback

You may also be challenged with new life costs—your first apartment, a new house, or a family. Little by little, you can begin paying down these investments. Be disciplined, manage your spending, and consistently apply some of your earnings toward these payments.

You may find yourself in a place where your desires are greater than your ability to financially support them. Live within your means. Many of your desires will be better fulfilled later, in your Apply or Produce stages. Be cautious of significant financial commitments and use this time to gauge your lifestyle costs. Are you a Starbucks latte-a-day person, or do you make your own coffee? It will feel good to make some money and keep it after working so hard.

The investments you made in acquiring your skills may be a significant burden to you or your family. This is a time to start paying back those investments.

SUMMARY

The Develop stage is when you take your skills and knowledge to the workplace. You'll gain confidence and will practice the skills you have acquired. This is a period of uncertainty, a time when you are gaining your financial independence and learning about the frustration of getting a job.

Start exploring the workplace, companies, institutions, or trades. You may find yourself changing jobs, roles, or industries to reach the right fit for you. You may also want to develop new skills. And you may feel pressure to balance a career with your life.

You are making new friends, changing cities, and starting life as an independent adult. Financially, you can start to pay back some of your investments you have made. Start small but start now.

Gain confidence and practice the skills you have acquired.

4 **ADAPT—**

Apply

Continue Your Journey

OK, now you're ready, right? Well, kind of. You may have your career aspiration determined, a company or institution you trust, and colleagues you like working with. If all this is true, you are well on your way to a successful career. Well done!

I find this stage to be the beginning of your career trip: you have a destination, but you need a map, gas, and money. You can take the expressway or the scenic route. Sometimes you can

You have a destination, but you need a map, gas, and money.

choose your route, other times you can't. Hopefully, you have managed your career and financials so you have options, and you can choose the appropriate path.

I became CEO of a medium-sized consulting firm at the age of 41. At that time, this was a relatively young age. I think I was given the CEO role because I was ambitious, carried no personal agendas, and managed the most important client to the firm. I had been with the firm for 12 years. Prior to becoming CEO, I held numerous roles within the organization. I would tell employees, "I had every role in the firm, except as a receptionist, which was way too stressful for me."

I did not aspire to be CEO, but I was motivated to develop a successful career. Fortunately, I found myself in a company and an industry that was growing rapidly and would offer me opportunities to grow.

The expressway, of course, offers the fastest way to your destination, but you will likely miss many sights and sounds available on your journey. Also, by driving too fast, you might make some small mistakes that can lead to significant consequences.

There are two routes you can take—the expressway or a scenic one—and they both have advantages and disadvantages.

Applying your skills patiently and deliberately to different jobs, assignments, or organizations can lead to a better appreciation of the challenges and commitments necessary to be successful. These roads might be less traveled, so getting stuck is always a potential. So, surround yourself with "tow trucks," including friends and family, that can give you a little push or pull when needed.

You will take one step at a time. You will need to focus on how each new opportunity fits into your overall career aspiration. Experimenting with roles is OK, but don't let these experiences distract you from building your career.

Critical to this stage is a confirmation of your company, your industry, and your chosen profession. Make sure you can grow your career in your company, and that your chosen profession remains meaningful.

Consider this stage as a time to project yourself forward. You don't want to stand still.

ASPIRATION 3

Picking Your Destination and Your Path

You are likely becoming very focused on your career. You are working with others who challenge and teach you. You may also see your "like" person—"I would like to be like Alicia or Derek." While you see successful people around you, you also see those who are "putting in the time and counting days." I suspect that if you're reading this book, you're not one of those. You are committed to growing your career and expect to do well.

You will now be taking small but important steps in your career. Given the number of opportunities you have, picking your ultimate destination may be difficult. Maintain connections along the way with those who have supported you and believe in you. This social capital with colleagues will help as you grow your career.

Confirm or challenge the aspirational statements you made in the Develop stage. Do they remain relevant? Do they align with your passions and your life goals? Are they achievable? Maybe you decide on an updated career aspiration. Wonderful! Now take the time necessary to further articulate your ambitions.

Next, build your career map. If you have your destination articulated, you will need a map to get there. Again, this map will change over time, but let's start by finding the route that's most realistic and achievable. Your ultimate path will depend on your life and your ambition. Your map can be as general or as detailed as you want. However, don't be discouraged if your journey takes some scenic routes along the way.

Some considerations as you build your career map:

⇨ What do I see myself doing in 15 years?

⇨ What do I see myself doing in 5 years?

⇨ What are the next three career opportunities I should seek?

⇨ Are there specific roles I need on my journey?

⇨ Can I reach my career ambitions in this company, this industry?

⇨ Are my mentors providing me the support I need?

⇨ What are my strengths and weaknesses?

⇨ Financially, can I provide for a lifestyle I desire?

> *Don't be discouraged if your journey takes some scenic routes along the way.*

TIDBITS
food for the soul

39—Map Your Route

On my path to becoming CEO, I had seven roles in 12 years. Did I have a "career map"? No, but the challenge of learning and applying new skills was exciting and very rewarding. It's important to conceptualize your career path. As you move forward in an organization, begin applying your skills and knowledge. Then, as with any trip, be open to your plans changing—sometimes for the better. So, don't be afraid to change your route.

> *The best path for you will become clear. Just keep your eyes on your destination.*

This also is an ideal time to seek support from your mentors. Get their advice on your ambition, the next steps, and the challenges that may lie ahead. Challenge yourself to seek roles and assignments that require new skills. If you've never had to face clients or customers, find a role that does so. If you've only been in

90

operations, find a role in marketing and sales. These new roles will help you build the skills, knowledge, and perspectives needed to advance your career.

40—Do Your Homework

You thought you were done with homework. No. It's time to apply those study skills to your career. Stay current with your career; learn about your organization. Take time to reflect and renew yourself. There are several questions you should ask. Is this an industry I can see myself in for the next 20 to 30 years? Are my career aspirations aligned with the potential offered by my current company? Should I change my "destination" and plan for a different career opportunity? Even though you may enjoy working in your organization, you should keep open-minded about other companies or institutions.

Hopefully your organization can fulfill your career aspirations. Use your knowledge of the organization to seek new assignments or roles consistent with the long-term goals of the company or organization. Take a new assignment in a new business unit, one that has the support of the organization to grow over the next years. Look at becoming part of a team looking into a new technology, service, or solution aligned with your organization's ambitions.

41—Take Career Steps

As you look at your career in this Apply stage, think of your roles in 12- to 18-month increments. I am a firm believer that it takes 4 to 6 months to learn your role, the expectations, and what you need to focus on to be successful. If or when you start managing people, it takes at least this long to understand individuals, their strengths and weaknesses, and what motivates them. In the next 8 to 12 months, you have an opportunity to demonstrate your effectiveness in the role, and that you're ready for a more challenging assignment to move your career forward.

Within each of your roles, find a way to "make your mark." In every job there are critical results that will allow you to continue to develop your career. As I grew my career, I took on the account management of our largest client. The client trusted me, and I was very committed to them and their success. The account grew significantly and allowed us as a firm to invest in diversification of the business and advance new service lines. Your "mark" may not be with client management, it might be advancing an important business initiative, developing a new way to manage treatment care, or inventing a new technology. A warning: you can always leave a negative "mark."

42—Make It a Job Well Done

Don't forget the obvious. In order to promote your career down the road, you need to execute in your job now. Regardless of your aspirations or your plan, performance needs to be embedded in your personal brand. Never underestimate a job well done. It is imperative to your success.

How do you perform at your highest level? First, be sure your assignment is clear to you and your manager. Agree on the desired results, the resources you have been given, and the authority you have to execute. If any of these items are misaligned, you may fail. Second, give yourself license to get the information you need to accomplish your assignment. Seek out those who may support you in determining the scope and facts behind your assignment. Last, be persistent. It is up to you to succeed, not others. If you accept an assignment, it is important that you follow through to completion. If you run into roadblocks, identify them early.

43—Keep Gas in the Tank

Whether you take the expressway or the scenic route, you will need plenty of gas—energy—to get you to your destination. Filling up can take many forms, and it is highly individualized. Some people like to find time for themselves, so they get away from the day-to-day routines and escape to reflect. Others may want to spend more time with family and friends, enjoying and growing nonwork relationships. If you are running out of gas, and no station is in sight, call on your mentor or your closest friend or family member. Those who know you best will likely give you the extra boost you need.

When I took my CEO role, the colleague whom I succeeded told me, "Don't run out of gas." For him, the job meant constant pressure and visibility. He was really an introvert but needed to be an extrovert for the role. He would often "charge his batteries" by isolating himself from the business to take time to think and reflect.

The key is to recognize what you get energy from, and what drains you. As you would expect, you can never avoid energy-draining experiences; just recognize and balance them with positive energy-gaining activities.

44—Take a Detour

As you manage your career, you are also living your life. Understanding how to balance both life and career can be increasingly difficult in this phase. Unexpected events like a layoff or a health issue may give you time to reassess your path and make the necessary changes.

It may be hard, but try to view these unexpected events positively. Take the time to evaluate your career, your path, and make positive changes. Also, you may take some planned detours. Have children, take a trip with a close friend, or fulfill one of your bucket-list items. If you don't take detours, you may find them to be a distraction in the future. "If I'd only..." Take the detour, but be sure you know the way back to your path.

Building your career is complex. Whether it is planned or not, sometimes a detour is helpful.

A colleague of mine is an avid out-doors enthusiast. He has managed to take extended sabbaticals to hike the Himalayas, raft the Grand Canyon, and back-country ski the Cana-dian wilderness. Other colleagues have taken tempo-rary roles with organizations that are aligned with their personal commitments, including political campaigns, international health organizations, and environmental land trusts.

45—Don't Get Stuck

What happens if you get stuck? Generally getting stuck occurs when your organization doesn't support you, you've chosen the wrong career, or you run out of gas.

Remember, you should be refueling when needed, but you should also assess your career ambitions and be sure they are aligned with your organization's opportunities. These evaluations can be difficult. You might really like the people you work with, but you don't like the organization. You may really like your job, but you don't see long-term career opportunities.

One solution: Engage your mentors, both internally and externally. Internal mentors can help you assess your organization's specific opportunities. External mentors can provide fresh perspective on your situation and perhaps size up opportunities outside your organization.

You may be able to access career development opportunities within your company. If so, seek assistance. If not, work with your mentor to reset your plan or renew your career by reentering your Acquire or Develop stage of your career life cycle. In some cases, it may be as simple as taking night classes to advance your degree or certifications necessary to compete.

The point is to get the support you need to help clarify your concerns, doubts, or challenges.

46—Professional Brand Matters

Whatever industry you choose, this is a great time to evolve your personal brand to your professional brand. Seek out and participate in industry associations, professional societies, and interesting conferences or trade shows. Generally, there are too many choices, and you will need help focusing on a key few industry forums where you can participate and establish yourself.

Believe it or not, I still maintain collegial relationships with people I met 35 years ago at industry outings. Start small, join local chapters, learn about the community, and develop to national- or global-level engagement as appropriate. If you can, present papers, offer to speak, facilitate panels, or offer yourself to subcommittees or planning sessions. It is a lot of work, and much of it will be on your personal time and expense, but it's worth it. You may eventually need helpful advice from an industry colleague; for example, if you are seeking new opportunities to advance your career. These contacts will prove especially useful.

Being recognized by your industry peers can be one of the highest achievements of your career. Your peers in these relationships know how hard it is to become the best in class. They will be critical, but also very supportive as you achieve your own personal goals.

47—Collegial Relationships Matter

Much like developing your industry network of relationships, always look for ways to develop your collegial relationships within your organization or institution. Like developing client relationships, use the "zipper approach" to create internal relationships. What's the zipper approach? Simply put, you want to build relationships with organizational peers, superiors, and subordinates.

You will likely have the most in common with your peers who work at the same level as you do. Those relationships should come easily. Find those you respect who will support you rather than compete against you for career advancement. (Although even a friendly competitor can be helpful.) Feel free to discuss your frustrations, share organizational news, and keep each other informed.

Never breach the trust with your peers, take credit for their work, or forget them as you advance your career.

Supervisors can provide a bigger picture of the organization and are always looking for the next "rising star." Pick these relationships carefully, though. Introduce yourself, make it a point to have an informal conversation, and recognize their organizational accomplishments. If comfortable, ask for routine meet-ings or semi-annual discussions. If appropriate, ask them to be your mentor.

Last, but certainly not least, build relationship with those "below" you. They may or may not report to you, but they have a unique view of the organization and can help you see your organizational blind spots. Test your leadership behaviors, support them by highlighting the benefits of the organization and the benefits they offer the organization, and be sympathetic to their con-cerns. Don't make their issues yours. Rather, help them problem-solve and develop their skills to be success-ful in the organization. Subordinates can positively or negatively influence decision-makers when it comes to career advancement.

48—Client Relationships Matter

Maybe one of the most important elements of the Apply phase is to begin or continue to develop your client relationships and networks. Clients come in all forms—internal clients, market clients and companies, patients, or members. Depending on your organization or insti-tution, clients are those people for whom you provide a service or a product. Generally, they are the ones who pay the bills, and ultimately your salary.

Where do you start? First, understand clearly those clients that are important to your organization and considered long-term and industry-leading. You will find out soon that not all clients are the same; you will have tactical clients and strategic clients.

I am a believer that all clients are good; however, some are better than others.

Second, become part of the client delivery team for those strategic clients. If you don't have a client-facing role, find one. Volunteer, or seek out a lead client role for execution or business development. If you are building a practice—a group of clients that you intend to "own" over time—start now and make it a priority.

Finally, target individual client relationships that you feel will last throughout your career. You will find later that your older client relationships will be retiring and passing the baton to the next generation of employees. Develop a good mix of client relationships—ones with a broad range of responsibilities, age, and status in the client organization.

Think of your client relationships as a garden: plant some of your relationships, and harvest others. Spend the time to care for your garden; you will be able to harvest a lot if you nourish and cultivate.

49—Organization Knowledge Matters

Remain curious about your organization or institution. Always seek knowledge of the organization's strategy, performance, and leadership. In today's world, organizations change frequently and quickly. Stay current with the organization's structure, key decision makers, future leaders, and new developments in service, technology, or products. A challenge is to stay relevant to the organization and remain a contributing member of the team. Insert yourself and take on assignments that may lead to future opportunities. Try to resist doing the same thing day in and day out.

Staying relevant is important. An organization's vision, mission, and strategies should be more than a sign on the wall or a blog from your CEO. These "organizational tools" are an attempt to clarify the future direction of the company and its investment priorities. Staying relevant means you can continue to craft your career to bring the requisite value to clients and the organization. Projecting your value to the organization can help you determine your next steps on your career path.

50—Work Through Others

You will soon learn, or maybe you have already, that you are turning from a player to a coach. Of course, you have your own personal accountabilities, but the organization needs you to do more. In order to build a long-lasting career, you will eventually need to lead, manage, and inspire teams. These teams will magnify your success if they are made of the right people, have clear goals, and are motivated to succeed.

This may be one of the most challenging steps in your career! For years you have been directed to do things: "wash the dishes," "clean your room," "finish your assignment tomorrow by noon," "produce your monthly report."

A how-to on leading teams is a book in itself! (There are many out there.) In simple terms, be sure you have the right people, the right "mission," and motivate the team to successful outcomes. Most people want to know why they should do something and what success means to them. The "why" is gener-

And now it's time to direct others to get the most out of your team.

ally the easiest: you want to tie everyone's assignment to the goals of the organization, make the assignments clear, and support the team members in achieving their goals.

"What's in it for me?" can be more challenging. This requires you to understand what your team members value and how success in these assignments will lead to the achievement of their personal goals. Take the time to help your team members make that connection.

51—Gee, You Are Wonderful

It's important at this stage to learn how to keep yourself motivated and confident. Everyone is different, but finding ways to build and enhance your self-esteem is critical. You will encounter failures, problems, and people who may like you—or not. Find your trigger, your anchor that will get you on track from a bad day, bad presentation, or some concerning words. Every day, you should walk away from your job feeling confident and successful. You should be able to reflect on your daily accomplishments and be proud.

I hate to admit this, but every morning as I got ready for work, I would look in the mirror and say to myself, "Gee, you're wonderful." This was my way to start off the day with a positive feeling about myself. And every day when I returned home, I would ask myself, "Did I earn my salary today?"

Silly rituals? Sure. But effective? You bet.

Start your day with confidence and end it with pride. Find your "gee, you're wonderful" trigger. It will come in handy. Really!

52—Dress the Part

What to wear to work? The organization will likely dictate what is acceptable clothing and what is not. Integrate your dress into your personal and professional brand. Dress slightly better than your colleagues, but never better than your clients. It is not a fashion contest, but you will want to support your brand and your aspirations with the way you look. If you have identified your next step, the next role in the organization, look around.

Your choice of dress will certainly leave a first, and possibly, a lasting impression. An Italian colleague of mine wanted me to take him to buy a pair of cowboy boots while he was visiting me in Houston. Cowboy boots? He said, "I want to dress like my American oil and gas customers when I meet with them."

Dress like those who are already in those similar positions.

Maybe a little extreme, but your dress should support your brand and help you relate to your colleagues and clients.

53—Know Who Makes Things Happen

In every organization, there are the doers—those people who understand how the organization operates and how to most effectively get the job done. Sometimes it is the obvious person—the one in charge. However, often it is not the person in charge but someone who has more institutional credibility.

Our leaders are expected to make numerous decisions on behalf of the organization. However, they can't make every decision; day-to-day actions are often delegated to their team and support personnel.

If the busses weren't running, there would not be any school.

Both of my parents were school administrators, serving as principals, superintendents, or headmasters for most of their careers. I remember my mom telling me that the most important people in the school leadership were her administrative assistant and the manager of the bus garage. If the busses weren't running, there would not be any school. If she did not want to see someone, her assistant had the key to her office door.

We have all experienced working with organizations and clients where the gatekeepers and the mission-critical teams manage the business. In your organization, these may be the IT team, the payroll processing group, HR benefits administration, contract attorneys, and/or the accounting/finance team. These functions and the people working in support of these functions control the pace of work and the responsiveness of the organization. This is where most organizations fail to realize your clients' needs.

Even more importantly, you should be asking who influences your client or leaders' decisions. I spent a career getting to know executive assistants, receptionists, and office managers. For every client contact I have, I also have their executive assistant's name, telephone number, and email address. In some cases, I even have their birthdays and kids' names. I wanted each of my key clients and organizational leaders to see me as a colleague—someone they could trust and wanted to spend time with. If their closest advisor was not on board, I would never get the call back, the meeting set, or my advice taken.

Find who influences the decision-makers of your clients and leaders.

Take the time to get to know the doers!

54—Don't Focus on Failures

It is human nature to focus on our failures and not celebrate our successes. If you believe in evolutionary psychology, it assumes that all human behaviors reflect the influence of physical and psychological adaptations that helped human ancestors survive and reproduce. Why is this important? If you subscribe to this theory, there are two important things we can do to survive. First, avoid the threats in our life. Secondly, when confronted with those threats, we cannot fail: it could be life or death!

Another example of our preoccupation with failure can be seen in the SWOT analysis you have done with teams in your organization. Based on some of my recent work with clients, the story remains the same.

It's human nature to focus on the failures and not celebrate our successes.

Generally, teams identify many more Weaknesses and Threats than Strengths or Opportunities. Why is that? We are protecting ourselves from failure by anticipating those things that could cause us harm.

While protecting ourselves from failure is important, it is equally vital to accept and learn from our failures; fear of failure can hinder creativity and innovation.

Alternatively, if we can identify our successes and celebrate them, we can build the confidence to experiment more, create more, and achieve our goals. A common mistake we make is to wait for the BIG success. However, it's up to you to define what success looks like and ensure your goals are achievable. Getting caught up on every failure is demoralizing and counterproductive, while celebrating the little successes along the way to the BIG success is rewarding and motivating. Also, when celebrating your successes, find those who have helped you to succeed. Maybe it's a family member, a friend, your partner, or a colleague at work. Sharing your success with others is a meaningful way of thanking them for their support.

Before I leave this Tidbit, a little more psychology. There is a term called "anticipatory rewards." Research suggests that we derive more pleasure from anticipating rewards and successes than the actual achievement itself. So why not celebrate the little successes along the way?

Fearing to fail hinders creativity and innovation.

55—Be Your Exceptional Self

Everyone has an exceptional self. Exceptional people have characteristics that allow them to be both effective and easy to work with. You have those characteristics, it's just a matter of finding them and letting them develop in the workplace. Ask yourself: when do I feel best about myself? What do I do that gives me energy and enlightens me?

Many of us, myself included, work on these characteristics daily. It's not enough to recognize your exceptional characteristics, you must work on them, use them, and fine-tune them. Developing your exceptional self is not limited to your work, but also your life. You will be successful and admired if you are effective at both work and life.

> What do I do that gives me energy and enlightens me?

Here are some of the characteristics that can support you in becoming your exceptional self. Be honest, be curious, be pleasant, be respectful, be effective and focus on what matters, at work and outside of work. Your ability to draw on your exceptional self will help you become successful in your career and your life.

Coming to work means more than just showing up. If you want a career that will reward you for your hard work, be the best you can be as soon as you arrive. If you were going to run a marathon, you would train for it, work out to remain fit, and meditate to stay in the moment. Why not think about work as an event you need to prepare yourself for? Find those things that allow you to be your exceptional self. Look for work assignments that challenge you, colleagues that you enjoy working with, and clients or projects that you find interesting.

Come to work ready to be successful.

Come to work to be successful. Deploy your exceptional self in the workplace and at home. It is far better to run the marathon after you have been running 10 miles a day for the last month than to jump in unprepared.

56—Morning-After Emails

Have you ever sent an email or text message to someone that you should not have? After exercising your better judgment, you wish you would have been more considerate, less emotional, and maybe it should not have been an email or text at all. Emails and texts are easy and generally very effective in keeping your colleagues or managers informed. I made it a rule that I would update my manager on a regular basis of where I was, what I was doing, and any client or organizational opportunities or challenges I was facing. If I needed help, I would ask for her support.

We all have our moments when we feel frustrated or discouraged. Then we get that email! A new policy, an ask for more effort, or just that irritating REPLY ALL email. I have to admit, I've made the mistake of RESPONDING IMMEDIATELY in ALL CAPS, expressing my disgust and handing out unsolicited advice. In the aftermath, I learned a lot. One thing I learned is that I was not fully aware of the issues the organization was facing or the challenges my colleague was having. I did not have the right context and I could have asked more questions if I was truly interested in the subject email. Secondly, in the grand scheme of things, the email wasn't a big deal.

> *Don't make the mistake of RESPONDING IMMEDIATELY with ALL CAPS!*

So, what should you do when you receive that irritating email or text? First, read it a couple times. The first time you read the message you could have been triggered by words or phrases that bias your interpretation of the email or text. Secondly, look for the key messages and any requested action in the email or text. Lastly, determine if the email or text is worth a response. Is it important to you or your assignment?

Now that you are ready to respond, let it rip! Put all your views, thoughts, and opinions in a response. However, don't send it yet. This is the critical part: send it to yourself first! Read your response later in the day or even the next morning. Now that you have spoken your mind, edit your response and leave constructive criticism or advice. Ask yourself, is this a message I could receive and consider valuable? If not, reconsider the reason you are responding at all.

> *Is this a message I could receive and consider valuable?*

57—The Best Jobs You Don't Apply For

As you develop your career, you will be seeking opportunities both within and outside your organization. I don't subscribe to, "It's not what you know, but who you know." If you don't need the skills and knowledge to land the job, you will need them to be successful. No matter your situation, it is only a matter of time until you will have to demonstrate your competence.

Organizations and their hiring managers look for people who have demonstrated the knowledge and ability to be successful within their profession. Entry-level roles are generally hired from the candidate's resume. Senior and leadership roles are hired because your effectiveness has been recognized by others. If you have embraced the Tidbits in this book, you are already on your way to getting your best job. Do you have a strong professional brand? Are you effective in your current role? Have you developed an industry network? Do you have a positive relationship with your mentors?

As I reflect on my career, all the senior level leadership roles I had were positioned by my relationships. One of my CEO roles was "won" by having demonstrated my commitment to the organization, managing the top client account, and gaining the trust of the founding partners. If I did not have the trust of the founding partners, I would have never been offered the role. Another CEO role was offered to me by an acquaintance from the little town we lived in. The industry was outside of my experience, but the owner had confidence in me to lead the firm. The last leadership role I achieved within my industry was offered to me after a brief interview. I had already been recommended to the hiring manager

You will be hired for entry-level roles because of your resume. You will be hired for leadership roles because your effectiveness has been recognized by others.

by an industry colleague who had worked with me several years prior.

The *takeaway* is that your demonstrated effectiveness is important. However, if you are not recognized or not trusted by others, the best job will go to someone else.

58—Work Will Not Love You Back

So, you give work your all—then what? We spend 40–50 years developing our career. We spend as much time working, if not more, than we do with our partner, friends, or children. They give you love back, so shouldn't work? No matter how you look at it, work is transactional. You earn the right to work every day.

You give your career your time, energy, commitment, and more, but what do you get back? Maybe you get challenge, financial flexibility, and recognition. Beyond that, what work can do is give you an opportunity to build a career that aligns with your life goals. Work will not love you back, but it can help you live a life you love.

Partner with your career to achieve your life goals.

As I mentor young career developers, I often hear, "I just don't love my work." I wish they did, but that's OK.

Some of my mentees see work as a foe, not a friend. Something they must do, not want to do. I get it, but try thinking of your work as a way to build a career, one that you can partner with to achieve your life goals. Sometimes we focus too much wondering, "Do I love my work," and not enough time asking, "Am I getting what I need from my career to support the life I want?"

Most people don't inventory the critical actions required to develop their career and achieve their life goals. That's a mistake. Once you stop seeing your work as something that will give you love, and instead see it as part of a career that will help you achieve a life you love, your partnership with your career will be far more successful.

Look for love from your family, friends, and partners— not your work!

Identify the critical actions you must take, set your priorities to leverage the things you are doing well, and enhance those things you could improve.

The long and short of it is, look for love from your family, friends, and partners—not your work!

59—Foster Confidence

Confidence is not something you can put on your resume, and yet having confidence in the workplace is important. If you want to grow your career, you will be faced with many new opportunities and challenges. Often you will be unprepared for what lies ahead of you. This is part of the fun, but it can also be intimidating. What will you do when you are presented with a situation you have not experienced before?

Blind confidence is dangerous, but measured confidence is an asset.

Blind confidence is dangerous, but measured confidence is an asset. Confidence comes from success; success comes from confidence and competence. Building confidence is a skill, both at work and in your life. Are you the first one to take on a new challenge, or the last? Seeing yourself as capable is as important as being capable. Confidence is the ability to draw upon your experience and skill to make decisions, even for new challenges.

Remove your doubt and give yourself a chance.

You are not born with confidence; you must foster confidence in yourself and others. Take on stretch assignments, learn a new language, travel and meet other cultures. Surround yourself with people who want you to be successful, remove your doubt, and give yourself a chance. Family, friends, coaches, and mentors are important team members in helping you gain confidence. You will fail, but it is how you learn from your failures and move forward that determines your success.

It's not enough to be confident—you also need to be capable. If you are both, you will exceed your own expectations.

60—Look for the Moment

There's a right time for everything. Your effectiveness, your success, and your passion for your career will not be consistent. There are times in your career where you have accomplished your goals and are ready to move on to more challenging roles. There are also periods in your career where you may need a break, a time to think and reposition your career or life. Recognizing these moments are important.

Position yourself for a YES.

When you need something different, leverage a period when you have been recognized for your success. Maybe you have recently completed an assignment critical to the team, maybe you just completed a new certification or degree program, or maybe you just made the big sale. Before you ask for that promotion, apply for that new role, or ask for a six-month sabbatical, be sure you have positioned yourself for a YES.

A moment will come when it's time to ASK. Assuming you have been successful, does your coach or mentor know of your intentions? Do you have a successor? Promoting yourself comes before the ASK. It is never easy to promote yourself, but it is important to achieving your career goals. It starts by looking for opportunities to excel, performing, and assuring that key decision makers know of your capabilities. It's a bit like putting money in the bank. You do it little by little, until you have the money you need to buy those things on your Amazon Wish List.

Promoting yourself comes before the ASK.

Don't assume everyone who needs to know about your capabilities and successes does. Sometimes your manager will be your best advocate, but not always. Be prepared when the moment comes and you make your ASK.

61—Know Your Financial Break-Even

You have made significant investments in your career and have begun to claw your way back into the black. Try to pay off your debt and put money away for retirement. You may already have done this, but if not, work hard to live within your means and free yourself from those financial handcuffs.

Know, too, that you may take on other financial obligations—a house, a family, or a new car. Plan now to fund these future investments. These will support your life moving forward.

One important step here: get a financial planner or someone who can coach you on how to protect yourself, your family, and build your long-term investment portfolio. Start to build your team of advisors—financial, legal, insurance, and general business. Look for people you trust ... those who are slightly older and ahead of you in building security and wealth.

You will want to learn from those who have been successful. They will give you comfort in making key financial decisions.

SUMMARY

The Apply stage is characterized by taking your skills and knowledge to a relevant industry, company, or institution. This job, in most cases, is just the beginning of your lifetime career. You may already have your career plan, but this stage helps you test, stretch, and confirm that you are on the right path. Embrace your strengths and your weaknesses, understanding that both are important as you develop your career.

This is a critical time for you to develop your professional network, your industry, and professional knowledge, and begin building relationships with your customers and key stakeholders. This stage may offer you the greatest challenge in how you manage your career pace. How fast or slow do you go in continuing to build your career? There may be a scenic route or an expressway; you can choose. Hopefully, this stage will allow you to pay off your career debt and focus on future investments.

5 ADAPT—

Produce

Be the Best You Can Be, Now!

This stage can be the most challenging phase of your career, but also the most rewarding. Expectations of you in the workplace and at home can be significant. You will need to be running hard, fast, and achieving your fullest potential in your career. Again, there are no fixed durations or ages in this model, but this is the time to make a full commitment to fulfilling your career

Challenge yourself to achieve your best and build a legacy you can be proud of.

ambitions and build financial flexibility for yourself to move forward.

My Produce years came to me quickly, at age 41, when I became CEO of a global environmental consulting firm. I didn't have a career plan, but I was lucky enough to be in a rapidly growing industry, surrounded with people who cared about me, and I was naive enough not to have any hidden agendas. My Produce period lasted about 20 years, but not without a few ups and downs. Some expected turns and some not so expected turns. The first 10 years of this stage were also very full of life, marriage, kids, family, restoring an old farmhouse, coaching, teaching, and being an elected official.

As I am sure you will find, your time is the most valuable thing you have in this stage of your career. Use it wisely.

You will be faced with many defining moments in your career. What satisfies my ambition? How do I balance my life commitments and a career? How long do I see myself doing this? Reaching your maximum potential will either come to you unexpectedly, or you will need to fight for it. I was in the right place at the right time, and I had the necessary ambition to be recognized and rewarded for my efforts. In other cases, you may have to experience some failures before achieving your maximum potential. Never give up. If you are confident and you have developed the right skills and behavior, you will find the right industry, organization, and role.

Ever play King of the Hill? Your Produce years are similar: getting to the top of the hill takes work; staying there may be even more difficult. As you develop your career, you will find

You will reach your maximum career potential.

that your success becomes more dependent on others and factors outside of your direct control. Your ability to motivate teams, expect excellence, and stay ahead of those things outside your control will determine the longevity of your success. You may be the best at what you do, but the market, your clients, or other business factors may change enough that your role or your function is no longer needed.

Maybe your success in one industry can be translated to another industry. You might see an opportunity with another company that suits your goals better than the current company. You may even seek a role with a company or firm to build other skills you need to advance forward or grow your career. However, keep a keen

Don't get fanatical or paranoid, just keep pushing yourself to learn and do more with your career.

eye on your goals and be confident that your moves will contribute to your longer-term success.

After being CEO for seven years, we sold our company and I resigned. I had a non-compete and could not work in my industry for three years. Fortunately, I had an opportunity to become CEO of a manufacturing company in the home construction market. Moving from a professional services firm and an industry I had known for 25 years was a challenge. Making this change helped me build confidence that I had the right skills to lead and manage firms outside my comfort zone. I also learned a lot about business management, family business, and—my favorite—banks. I was happy with my move. It taught me lessons I could take forward into a new role after my non-compete expired.

Reaching the top of your potential is only relative; there is always a new hill to climb, a mountain top to conquer. Once you get on top, rest and enjoy the vista, but never get complacent or take anything for granted. You are in an accelerated time zone that moves very fast, and you need to catch up and stay ahead!

> *This period should not be stagnant. It should be the most dynamic time of your career.*

ASPIRATION 4

Seizing the Moment

By now you are well on your way to achieving your career aspiration. You have narrowed your focus, built you career road map, and are well on your career journey. Your desired ambitions may be met by now. Challenge yourself to achieve your best and build a legacy you can be proud of. Put yourself at the end of your career and ask yourself, did I have a career and a life well lived?

Defining a successful career is more than having a strong and clear career aspiration. As you suspect, it is much more difficult than that. Define your life and career goals clearly and assess your progress routinely. As mentioned earlier, a successful career can support your life and help fulfill your life goals. Work to live, not live to work.

Be bold and seek opportunities to advance your career. You deserve every opportunity that may be presented to you. Cement your personal and professional brand and develop your own leadership style. Your colleagues are important, so support those who support you.

It is natural for you to ask yourself if this is what I want to do to the end of my career. Your view of your career may be changing. On the other hand, you may be fully satisfied with the people you work with and the benefits you're bringing to the community and your family.

Either way, you want to ask yourself, "What else can I achieve or do that will help others?" This may be volunteering, running for a public office, or coaching your favorite sport. You could argue these are not career aspirations, but they could lead to more satisfaction at work or at home.

Your career journey has been hard work, so honor yourself by achieving all your career and life aspirations.

TIDBITS
food for the soul

62—Use Your Judgment

All these years, you have been building your knowledge, your skills, and your ability to learn with an organization or industry. You now can get out your play book and call the plays you've wanted to call for years. You may be the boss, the senior member of your team, or the go-to technical resource in the organization. Your position gives you a lot of freedom. Also, there are a lot of eyes on you as you move the organization forward.

I remember as I was developing my career, a hiring manager told me, "Paul, we are not hiring you for your resume, we are paying you for your judgment." This became one of the best pieces of advice I'd ever received. I had spent a lifetime, or so it seemed, developing my skills and knowledge, and now I was being told it's just my judgment that counts. I learned very quickly

Be careful and use your success wisely.

that it is impossible to "learn" everything; you will never have all the information needed to make every decision. You will rely on your judgment more and more as you advance your career. Your judgment integrates the complicating and competing factors so you can reach the best decision for your team and your organization.

To help develop confidence in your judgment, work on projecting the likely outcomes from your decisions and actions. Over time, as these prove correct, you will gain more confidence in your judgment.

63—Lead With Your Behavior

One of the greatest differentiators of leadership is how a leader behaves. It is not enough in today's world to achieve the desired results; it is equally important to understand and articulate how you achieved the results you did. Behaviors also create and reinforce trust and an effective organizational culture.

Take the time to assess the decision or action in the context of the situation and the longer-term impacts to your team and your brand.

As you develop your career, you will occasionally see behaviors among your subordinates that seem to run counter to the culture of the organization. Resist a knee-jerk reaction, though. Instead, move the conversation forward.

Every day you will have challenges that require your attention and your calculated response. Remember, the words you use, the attitude you exhibit, are as important as that tough decision you need to make. As with your personal and professional brand, find the leadership behaviors that you can comfortably and consistently demonstrate to the organization.

64—Higher, Not Longer

Take a look at your organization. It's quite likely that the key leaders and producers have been in their roles for less than three years. Your "role longevity" can be very short. An organization needs to evolve and develop a bench strength to move the business forward.

In addition, successful people are asked to do many things in a short period of time. If you are good at leading people, you may also need to be good at creating a research and development organization. If you are good at sales, you may also need to be good at shareholder relations.

Look at this as the ultimate career challenge: You should stay slightly ahead of your potential while always seeking new challenges.

Reaching your career aspirations will likely involve several successful roles within an organization or across several organizations. As you would expect, staying at the top of your career is as difficult as getting there. It requires you to perform consistently over a period of time…years, in fact.

65—Make Your Mark

Whether you are CEO or a senior person in your organization, you must set a clear vision, desired outcomes, and your expected behaviors. There are many books written on mission- and vision-setting, but suffice it to say, keep yours short, understandable, and achievable. Why are we here, what do we want to achieve, and how do we behave?

Another way to express your intentions is to define your workplace DNA; what is it that defines you and what do you expect from others? Be sure you express what behavior you expect and what people can expect from you. This helps set the stage for trust and commitment. Every day, reflect on your behaviors and be sure they align with your stated expectations. If your behaviors are aligned, trust will happen; if not, it won't.

Making your mark is characterized by your accomplishments but also how you are perceived by your colleagues and your organization. It's critical to have trusted advisors in the organization who can inform you on how you are perceived. Take the praise and the criticism seriously, and use the information to enhance the mark you make.

66—A+ Team

It's easy to see that the best athletes make a team better. Same with successful organizations. What do sports organizations do? They identify key roles and fill them with the best people, compatible with the organization's culture. You need to do the same as you build a team, an organization, or a business. It is not easy to lead a team of high performers, but it is critical to your success. Be prepared to be challenged and accept that such challenges help you to improve yourself and the organization. You want your team to push you.

It can be hard to know if you have the right team. If you have the wrong team, it's a bit easier to identify. How do you know you have a high-performing team? You consistently meet or exceed your targets, are always challenging each other to do better, and the manner in which you achieve your results is consistent with the organizational culture. When you are operating at your peak performance, you are not only proud of your accomplishments, but also how you achieved your goals.

67—Reduce Complexity

As you elevate in your career, you will be asked to take on more complicated assignments. Such assignments can have longer durations, ambiguous outcomes, and numerous conflicting pressures. You are given these assignments because you're known for seeing the big picture, being highly motivated, and being very dependable at achieving results. It just gets harder, that's all.

You will find that if you can make the complex simple, you will get more from your team and the organization.

The complexity of the role is your problem, not your team's. Take on the complexity and support your team by keeping the most complex issues to yourself; transfer less-complex assignments to your team. Strong leaders can communicate the required actions necessary to reach more aspirational goals, and what it means to the individual. Your team must be able to connect the organization's aspirations with their own goals. Remember, your success is dependent more than ever on your team. That starts by keeping it simple.

68—Meaningful Metrics

Of course, the measurements should be aligned with the organization's desired outcomes and should be achievable. Make your metrics as meaningful as possible—those that truly contribute to the success of the organization. Metrics provide you and your team with guideposts that focus and direct

Developing the measurements of success is critical.

your resources and actions. Occasional "organizational noise" can distract you; use clear metrics to refocus and eliminate the noise.

Every organization expects more every year. Raising the bar is an expectation, but be careful about how you do it. Establish an understanding of the long-term ambitions of the organization, and create a road map showing how you will get there year after year. If you show your success in the context of your long-term goals, it will not seem so unrealistic. Test yourself and your team's ability to raise the bar incrementally before you commit to the organization.

Set yourself up for success. Develop goals you and your team can achieve. Meeting your goals can create the necessary momentum and confidence to generate even better results. But setting unrealistic goals—through unrealistic metrics—can only assure failure and destroy the confidence of your team.

69—Celebrate Success

It is not in everyone's character to celebrate the successes, but also don't dwell on the failures. As you move through your Produce years, take time to celebrate the successes. As you push yourself to do more and achieve more, give yourself and the team the occasional pat on the back.

A younger mentee of mine was so excited one day to let me know that her manager had made it a point to say "thank you" after she had completed a draft client report. I asked her what it meant to her. She said, "I worked hard on the report and his thank you helped me feel what I had done was important and my efforts were appreciated. I guess putting in the extra effort is worth it!"

Besides having fun and giving thanks, celebrating the successes also reinforces your expectations and your commitment to the organization. The most powerful words from you can be "thank you for a job well done." Never take these moments for granted, and be sure you recognize the primary contributors. This is the easiest thing you can do to advance your career and others.

70—Earn Your Keep

You are the best judge of your effectiveness and your overall contribution. Assure yourself that you are earning your role, title, and compensation. If you feel you can do more, speak up and take on more assignments. If you're not contributing enough, make the changes necessary to fix that.

Be honest with yourself about your role by routinely testing your value to the organization.

I made it a habit of doing this self-assessment at the end of each workday. After I parked my car and walked to the house, I would ask, "Did I earn my keep today?" My walk was only about 30 seconds, but I could always answer yes or no. If I had gotten sidetracked or failed to focus on the important things at work, I would likely answer no. If I had achieved my daily tasks and actions, I would decide on yes. Use your own measurements and your own judgment. Regardless, your answer will help you become more effective.

71—Balance Your Decisions

Understanding that every organization has its own values, behaviors, and expected norms, you need to develop an easy way to analyze and balance them for maximum effect.

Generally, organizational norms fall within four categories: best for the client or customer, best for the employees, best for the shareholders, and best for the community. Think of it as juggling four balls in the air and you can't let any hit the ground.

For example, one day you may have to decide between a termination and satisfying an unhappy client. I once had such a case. A client had awarded us a substantial contract but wasn't satisfied with our assigned account manager and wanted him removed. While we could obviously satisfy our client's expectations by reassigning the manager, how could we also satisfy the manager's expectation of our organization?

After extensive conversation with the employee, I realized he did not value the account manager assignment. We were able to create a role for him as a technical advisor, which was better aligned with the client's and employee's expectations.

72—Stay Connected

Assuming your career has allowed you to take on several different assignments, and you have numerous colleagues that you have worked with or for, these people are likely to be critical stakeholders in your ongoing success. Your network of colleagues, particularly in your current organization and in subordinate roles, can help you with your blind spots, provide valuable information, and help you effectively implement decisions.

One of your greatest challenges will be to gain alignment of the organization or your team to effect change. Of course, you may be good at strategy development, organizational diagnosis, and delivering desired outcomes. However, are you good at translating organizational needs to the individual level? Answering the question, "Why does this matter to me?" will be key to your success in driving the desired change.

Your colleagues, friends, and team members can help you understand the impacts of your decisions and how to most effectively communicate them.

73—Recharge Your Batteries

What is it that you get energy from? Is it a hobby, exercise, yoga, spending time with family and friends? Or is it reflecting on life on a sunny beach somewhere?

The Produce stage of your career will take a lot of time and energy from you. It may seem that you are living for work, not working to live. The last-minute deadlines, the uber-demanding client, or the difficult personnel decisions may all be building up. Whatever the pressure of work, you need a way to stay fresh and approach each day with enthusiasm and commitment.

How you recharge your batteries is obviously your decision. Working harder and working longer hours is likely not the best choice. You may seem like you are "getting things done," but if you were to step back and inspect, you can probably achieve the same results with a little ingenuity and be more effective.

Stay prepared during your career to be refreshed, creative, and focused on the most important actions to achieve your desired results.

Recharging will help you focus on the important things and eliminate organizational noise. If everything is important, then nothing is important.

74—Have You Developed Your Life Plan?

This is a great time to reflect on your long-term life plan. What will come after you are done working? Will you escape to an uncharted desert island or reinvent yourself into another long-lasting career? The possibilities of life after work are endless, but starting to narrow the list can help keep your current career path in perspective and make your expectations clearer.

Of course, your life plan will evolve over time. You can and certainly will refine your plans as you get close to the Transition stage of your career, but having a rough framework of your after-career goals is a great place to start.

Your plan could be as simple as deciding how long you want your career to last, what hobbies you have or want to develop, and maybe where you'd like to live once you are free from an office or other work location. Put the plan in your top left-hand drawer or on your hard drive in a file called "Life Plan." Look at it a couple of times a year and remind yourself why you are working so hard.

75—Reaching Your Destination: Are You Satisfied?

Having a successful career can be very rewarding, but it does come with challenges. Your life outside work and your relationships with others and your family can all be victims of a successful career. It's important that you pause and ask yourself, are you satisfied with your career and your life? Answer honestly and you will be able to move forward with confidence and commitment. You may be satisfied generally with life outside work but you still haven't reached your career aspiration. Adversely, you may have reached your career ambition but aren't satisfied with the life you lead.

It's a balancing act, and it's natural to have your ups and downs as you judge. The answers to your questions also can change day-to-day, year-to-year. It's a bit like dressing for the weather; sometimes you're hot and sometimes you're cold. Regardless, these are personal questions that only you can answer.

This balance is important. Consider again that you have about 40 years in your career. Spend them wisely, with no regrets...no "should haves." On either side of the ledger.

76—Meetings Make Me Dizzy

How many hours have you spent in meetings? Over my career, I estimate I have spent 25,000 hours in meetings—and this is on the lower end of my estimates. This is equal to 3,000 eight-hour workdays, or more than 10 work years. But that's just for me. By definition, meetings take place with others. Now think about the time spent in meetings by all your colleagues, managers, and leaders. How is that possible? Meetings have become

I have spent 25,000 hours in meetings, how about you?

part of ordinary business practices in most organizations. Meetings have become expected, assumed, and seen as a good use of our time.

I found that one positive effect of COVID was that meetings became more purposeful. Organizing and planning a meeting took more effort during COVID with teams working remotely. The meeting host now has to manage different time zones, flexible work schedules, and reliable conference video connections. The days where you could stroll down the hallway and organize an impromptu meeting are gone. But given that we still spend time in meetings, we need to ensure they are effective.

When I facilitate a meeting, I am focused on making the best use of the participants' time. I always calculate the cost of everyone's time, including the expenses and distraction of not being with clients or other team members. The most important takeaway is that meetings are costly! If you are in charge of a meeting, here are some recommendations:

First, start with a clear purpose and a list of your desired outcomes. The purpose should be easy to define. Outlining the desired outcomes does not mean that you want the meeting to turn out a certain way, but that specific decisions are made or assigned.

Second, ALWAYS have an agenda. Even if the meeting's purpose is team building, having an agenda will help maintain a good tempo, purposeful direction, and ensure that all your items to discuss or decisions to be made are addressed. Make it relevant to everyone—if it isn't, you have the wrong people in the meeting.

Third, start on time and finish on time (or slightly ahead of time!). Set the expectation that everyone's time is valuable and honor that with effective and efficient time management. Accomplishing a meeting's desired outcomes and ending early is a gift!

Lastly, get everyone involved either with pre-meeting assignments, facilitated discussion during the meeting, or post-meeting assignments. Making it real for everyone is important to engaging the team and driving results.

> *Accomplishing your purpose and desired outcomes and ending early is always a gift!*

It makes me dizzy to think about how much time people spend in meetings and the cost of this seemingly normal business practice. Make your meetings worth the effort!

77—Words Matter

Texts and emojis can make it seem like words don't matter anymore, but they do. Being precise with your language is an art form that many of us take for granted. It isn't so much about being careful, it's about being clear and compassionate. Some people like to fill the air with words, but if they aren't meaningful words, they're pollution. Words should be measured, not counted.

Words should be measured, not counted.

The less you say, the more you will be heard. In some organizational cultures, the loudest person is the one who is listened to. In learning and collaborative organizations, everyone's words are important. Don't be that person who needs to answer or respond in every situation. Don't be that person that talks over others just to make your point of view heard. Effective conversation in the workplace is extremely important to innovation and to optimal performance. How can you innovate if not everyone is engaged and one person is consistently pushing their view? How can you reach your optimal performance if you are always being told what to do, not being asked what you need to be successful?

In my facilitation of meetings, I find that the "quietest" people can sometimes be the most insightful. The trick is to give that person enough space and time to voice their opinions. Also, I find the most talkative people repeat themselves to be sure they have all their points covered. I am not encouraging you to stay quiet, but I am encouraging you to find the right words to express yourself with confidence and with meaning. Be prepared to express your opinions concisely while respecting the person or team you are speaking with. Use inviting and positive words: "we can," "let's all," and "have we thought about." These words will encourage people to listen and not be offended.

The less you say, the more you will be heard.

When you speak, you want to be listened to, not just heard.

78—The First 90 Days

The first ninety days is often your window to make a good "first impression" with the organization or your teams. As you accept new roles in an organization, you are expected to do great things. You have been hired or promoted because you have the confidence of the organization, your manager, or your team. You should be aware that everyone is watching to see how you behave, what your expectations are, and what will change or remain the same.

It is unrealistic to think that you will become completely effective or competent in the first 90 days. It is also unlikely that you will have your vision, your strategies, or your plan ready to roll out. However, you can make small changes to set the tone for how you will perform, behave, and lead moving forward.

You have 90 days to earn the confidence of your organization, manager, or teams.

Now for a short story. I replaced the Vice President in an organization that I had formally reported to. My frustration with him was that he would never return my calls in a timely manner. So, the first thing I did was set a rule for myself to return all calls I received from my team within two hours. I did not need to tell anyone about my rule, I just did it. This simple act was my way of reflecting my respect to the team.

While this is a positive example, there have also been instances when I waited too long to make change, or when I've made changes that were obvious to me but not to the rest of the team. As you move into your new role, do your due diligence. Find out what is working and what is not. It sounds simple, but remain clear-headed and consider all the

Do the small things that show respect, create expectations, or build engagement.

possibilities for improvement. Think of all the small things you can do immediately after accepting a new role to show respect, create expectations, or build engagement.

79—Manage Numbers, Lead With Behaviors

Managing and leading are both important, but they are certainly not the same. To me, managing involves organizing, assigning, and monitoring work to ensure it's executed. You manage your calendar, assignments, tasks, and deliverables. You lead people, change, and teams. Managing focuses on the present and near term. Leading is about being present, but focusing on the future. Managing can lead to short-term results; leading leads to sustainable results.

> *Leading is about being present, but focusing on the future.*

During your career, you will find people who are good managers, but poor leaders. You will also find good leaders who struggle as managers. Sometimes it is hard to be both. Organizations thrive when the culture supports achieving both the near-term and the long-term goals—solving today's challenges while remaining committed to capturing future opportunities.

When you become focused on the present, the organization focuses on production and administration. Near-term results can be numerous, including resource utilization, pricing margins, number of clients served, renewed funding, or quarterly share price. Of course, the near-term results are important and will allow the organization to honor commitments to clients, employees, and shareholders. Organizations that are committed to the future will foster creativity through promoting an entrepreneurial spirit and building systems for a sustainable culture.

Choose your behaviors and think long term while delivering on today's results.

The time you spend producing today's results or creating future opportunities is often inherent to your role. The organization will also cycle through their priorities, balancing today's and tomorrow's commitments. Choose your behaviors and think long term while delivering on today's results. When you are buried in a spreadsheet or are about to see your 20th patient, remember the big picture. If you believe in the organization's long-term goals, demonstrate your commitment by your behaviors.

People follow leaders who are committed to the future.

80—Lead With Your Heart

We are led to believe that the smart people get ahead, and that you have to be smart to be a good leader. The truth is that being smart is helpful, but having a respect for the people you work with and those who you lead will achieve more than being the smartest person in the room. Using your brain at work is important, but using your heart drives results.

Using your brain at work is important, but using your heart drives results.

If you research what characteristics are most valued in a leader by their teams, they are: Honesty, Competence, Inspiring Others, and Forward Looking. Teams respond best to leaders who are smart (competent) but also understand the behaviors required to engage and motivate teams.

Honesty, Inspiring Others, and being Forward Looking are traits that come from the heart, not the brain. It's easy to say that you're honest, but are you really? Your brain might tell you that you should be honest, but it is your respect for yourself and your team that convinces you to be honest. This is your heart speaking.

Have you ever been around a leader who tries too hard? The overzealous leader who tries too hard to be inspiring is leading with their brain. Those who sincerely want to inspire and are inspired themselves lead with their heart.

Looking forward to the future and setting the direction of the organization is an expectation of all leaders. While this takes knowledge of the business, the industry, and the markets, it also requires a commitment to change. How many of us have struggled to change our weight, our unhealthy habits, or even our daily routines, even if we know we need to? Change is driven by a strong desire, and desire comes from the heart.

We have all seen effective leaders, people who are smart but can also drive performance through others. That is why you are selected as a leader: you can accomplish more through others than you do individually.

> *Change is driven by strong desire; desire comes from the heart.*

81—Remind Yourself You Are a Leader

We all have leadership characteristics that will help us in our careers and our life. What are yours? Leadership is often defined as guiding and inspiring others, but leadership starts from within. Begin by guiding and inspiring yourself. Build your career and life aspirations, develop your plan, and guide yourself to success.

Whether you are guiding and inspiring yourself, a team, or an organization, you are a leader. Whether you want to "lead the parade" or just "go for a ride," leadership requires passion; if you have passion for what you do, you will be able to lead yourself and your teams to success. Sometimes you may question your leadership, you may be tired of the fight, or feel overwhelmed by the fact that people are depending on you. Accepting leadership is the first step to effective leadership.

Begin by guiding and inspiring yourself.

Everyone is born to be a leader. However, we are not always given the opportunity to lead, nor do we always see ourselves as leaders. Remember: we are built to survive. Our world is full of danger, and we are threatened daily by life's challenges. We choose to make decisions every day, whether it is to bring an umbrella, cross the street, accept a new role, or go on the first date. The decisions we make guide our career and life outcomes; you are showing leadership every day, even if you don't realize it.

Leadership should be an honor, not an obligation.

Leadership should be an honor, not an obligation. Leading yourself or others to success can be one of the most rewarding experiences you will ever have. Find those leadership characteristics that you have, the ones you value in yourself, and use them to be successful. Reflect on your life and the decisions you have made to find inspiration and confidence in your leadership capabilities.

Remind yourself that you are a leader and that you can guide and inspire others.

82—Keep It Simple

I am sure you have heard, "keep it simple!" It's good advice. Whether it is in your career or in your life, minimize complexity and keep it simple. Some people prefer complexity, and that's OK, but don't expect everyone to jump on board with you and explore the complexities of your career or life. Humans are the smartest animals on Earth, but our ability to process, connect, and act on complexity is limited. This is not anyone's fault; it is just the way we try to keep ourselves safe and protected for our future.

Keep assignments simple.

In a classic business framework, organizations should be structured so that leadership, management, and executive teams are addressing the most complex challenges of the organization. Questions such as, "What will the needs of our clients be in 10 years?," "How will a changing workforce affect our business?," "How will technology accelerate our success?," or "Will regulatory changes affect our business?" are critical to answer. These challenges are complex, and depending on how they are addressed, will enable the organization to flourish or lead to its organization decline. Obviously, Kodak did not get the camera right. Did Microsoft get software right? Organizations must prepare themselves for the future or risk a premature death.

The consequences of not addressing these complex issues are dire. However, of equal importance is the need to simplify the organizational response to these influences. The art of delegation is not just to free up your plate so you can do more work, but also about keeping the most complex elements of your assignment to yourself and simplifying assignments for your team. Simplified assignments are easier to execute, and if aligned with your role, they will efficiently address the critical challenges or opportunities the organization is facing.

As a manager, provide the why, not the how.

If you are a manager giving assignments, provide the context necessary for your team to understand the "why" and delegate simple, achievable assignments to your team. If you are an employee receiving assignments, be sure you understand the assignment, how success will be measured, and ask for the resources you need to achieve the desired goals.

83—Speak to What Could Be

Describing today's reality is easy. You look around, you gather information, and you create a story about who you are, what the organization does, and how things can be better for you and the organization. Knowing who you are and where you have come from is important. It's the same with your organization: how did it all start, what has happened over the years, and who were those great people you used to work with? Being present is critical to appreciating the challenges and opportunities you may face. However, it is only half the story. Creating stories about the future can energize and move your career forward or improve your organization.

> *Describing today's reality is easy. Taking a future-facing view of your career or your organization is hard.*

Taking a future-facing perspective of your career or organization is hard. It requires being curious and interested in creating a new reality for yourself and your organization. Visualizing your career and the organization's future will help you change your behaviors to achieve your future aspirations. What can you do today to make tomorrow more achievable? Do you need to learn a new skill, get a new role, or change your career aspiration?

Try an experiment with a colleague or manager when you have a chance. When your colleague or manager is telling you how things are, take an opportunity to describe to them how you think things could be and why that would be so much better. See if they will engage with you to expand on your ideas and become excited about the future. I call this the "what if we." Give yourself, your colleagues, and your managers a glimpse into the future.

Balancing the realities of today with the possibilities of the future is challenging. However, if you are seen as someone who understands the current realities and can present yourself or your organization an exciting view of the future, you will prove your relevance and your excitement will spread.

Speak to what could be, not what is!

84—Financial Accumulation

I'm hopeful that during your Produce phase, you are not only producing for your organization but for yourself as well. You will have a life to live after work, and it's important you prepare for it. Your expectations of compensation, benefits, and future savings needs are unique and will require a plan. Of course, personal issues can disrupt your plans, but take time throughout your career to secure your financial future.

How much can you earn, how much should you spend, and how much can you invest for the future? Your earnings potential is a combination of your career aspiration and your ability to create value. It is up to you to maximize that potential. So, continuously assess your value and ask to be fairly compensated.

You're also in control of your spending, and you can accumulate both wealth and stuff. Buying stuff is fun, but will you need that same stuff at age 65?

The key: invest as much as you can and as wisely as you can. Build yourself some financial flexibility.

SUMMARY

The Produce stage can be challenging, but also may be the most rewarding. You will need to run hard and fast to achieve your fullest potential. This phase will have a finite duration, likely 20 to 25 years, and you should make the most of it. You may feel more alone than ever as you lead a team, a business, or your own company. At the risk of sounding morbid, this is also when you write you career eulogy.

Expectations of you in the workplace and at home can be significant. You will need to find ways to keep your batteries charged and a clear focus on the important things. Maybe most important, your judgment and behaviors will create a lasting impact on the organization and your career. This is a time to accumulate wealth and guarantee some financial flexibility.

6 ADAPT—

Transition

Retire or Reinvent

Transition is the time to consider changing a career or ending one. You will spend considerable time during this stage reflecting on your career, your accomplishments, and any unfulfilled aspirations. You'll likely have some unfulfilled goals by this stage, but in the balance of life and career, you should have few regrets. You should be enthusiastic about what comes next.

So, how to proceed? Usually the most challenging part of this stage is the "when." When do you begin winding

Start checking items off that bucket list.

down your career or take the chance to reinvent yourself? These aren't small decisions. This could mean leaving the workforce you've known for decades, including leaving a big paycheck.

The other key question is "what." What kind of life do you now want to lead? You may prefer to be insular—retire and reside in a cabin reading books, watching Netflix, and going to the grocery store just once a week. Or you may want to bust free—retire and see the world, be completely spontaneous, reconnect with far-flung family and friends. Start checking off items on that bucket list.

"What?" can also mean reinvention. Perhaps fulfill a lifetime passion of helping people. Or take your skills to another industry, company, or organization. Or be your own boss and run a small business.

If you choose to reinvent, good luck!

It's an exciting time. Basically, you are returning to your earliest career stages, but with a significant difference: you have considerable skills and knowledge to bring to the job. Don't be afraid to take risks ... to experiment. Sure, reinventing yourself can be difficult, but if you have a clear vision, you will succeed.

As you decide these questions, take the time to listen to friends, family, partners, and colleagues. They are good sounding boards. They see you from a different perspective. For example, you may be in denial about how much your career means to you—that you would be lost without one. You may also have colleagues who recently retired or reinvented themselves. Tell them what you are thinking, and seek their advice. Learn from their examples.

If you are alert, your company or organization may start giving you clues about your value and place within it. Sometimes the message can be very direct: "Say, Paul, have you developed your succession plan?

Usually, you are not fully in control of this Transition stage.

Your role is important, and if you are planning to retire soon, perhaps it's time to map that out for us internally?" This is your opportunity to recognize a clear organizational message that you have a limited career life left in the organization. It also helps you control your own fate.

Or the company can take a more subtle approach. It may look past you when new business opportunities arise, or promote someone younger to an important position. Or it may change its direction or business model without consulting you first. Often, these actions aren't directed at you in a negative way, but instead reflect the reality of your career stage and the organization's strategic needs. You want to be alert to these subtle changes and approach them proactively, not reactively.

Ideally, you will be able to decide when and how to transition.

159

In some cases, your choices will be clear—say, in the form of a reduction in staff or an early retirement program. In other cases, the organization may be waiting for you to decide on your next step ... that succession plan.

If you retire, you are likely leaving a company and an industry that you've known forever. You also are leaving colleagues who have supported and challenged you throughout your career. You are losing your title, power, influence, and many of the other benefits you get from having an active career.

But let's look at what you gain. You no longer face those tough client or employee conversations. You get the freedom to control your daily schedule. You can, at last, freely and fully celebrate the family birthdays, anniversaries, and other important milestones without work getting in the way. Just as important, you have a new freedom to fulfill other interests and passions.

Whatever you decide—retire or reinvent—do it on your terms and not on the terms of others. You've earned that right.

Of course, a significant controlling factor in your decision to retire or reinvent will be having the financial flexibility to choose that path. As I've stressed in the prior stages, you need to be continually building the financial foundation that will now allow you to transition.

ASPIRATION 5

Stratified, but What's Next?

Maybe the term career aspiration at this stage of your career is a misnomer. Maybe a better way to look at it is, "Am I satisfied? If yes, what is next?" Considering these questions while you are employed can be challenging. Finding the time to renew your life goals, your new business plan, or your financial plan takes time. Try your hardest to protect the time you need to consider all your options.

You may have fulfilled your career ambition, but have you fulfilled your life's ambition?

To be realistic you may also be considering how much time you really have. We would all like to live to be a hundred, but the chances of that are not in our favor. The time you have left no longer seems endless, and you no longer feel as invincible as you likely did in your 20s or 30s. You may have fulfilled your career ambition, but have you fulfilled your life's ambition?

Step back, inventory your career and life, and be selfish of your time. If you are still young or interested in starting a business, develop a business plan. If you are interested in retiring, develop a retirement plan. Regardless of the path you take, keep your life goals in front of you and take on the world.

TIDBITS
food for the soul

85—What Will You Miss Most?

I remember when I was contemplating a career transition and I was asked by my sister-in-law, "What will you miss most if you leave your job or when you retire?" I responded, "My paycheck and my Diamond Medallion flight status."

Based on my response, it's pretty clear where I was in my decision-making, right? If I was ambivalent about leaving, I could have answered: "The challenges of my job, my colleagues, and the excitement I get from having a meaningful purpose in my work." Instead, emotionally, I had already moved on.

Once you move on, though, be careful. Depending on your job and your organization, it is important to stay committed.

Don't disconnect and disengage. Also, don't move on until you have a clear plan on how and what you will transition to.

Clearly understanding what you will miss from your career is important. It is a very direct question to help focus on why you are working now and why in this role. Obviously, there are no right or wrong answers; it depends on how you view you career, your job, and your commitment. It can also be very helpful in framing your transition to a new career or to retirement.

What is it that you are looking for in a transition? What will be important when I leave or retire? Try to imagine a new career or retirement. Go into your Transition with eyes wide open.

86—Be Alert to Macro Trends

In today's society and business, time moves faster and faster. Your organization has been built to address your customers' needs—whether products or services. But your organization is also driven by current norms, expectations, technology, and social interests. Obviously, these factors change with time ... some very fast, others more slowly. Sometimes these trends can accelerate beyond our skills and knowledge, and your career path may need to change. Being aware of these macro trends, and understanding how your organization or business will respond, will affect you and your career.

It's not always easy to monitor these trends. An example is today's energy transition—the speed with which we adopt alternative energy and the acceptance of electric vehicles. That will ripple through industries worldwide. It will impact our lifestyles, too.

How these macro trends affect your business is best monitored by the vision and strategies your organization sets for the long term. Maybe your company is becoming a wholesaler, not a retailer. Maybe your company is changing from a hardware company to a service provider. Regardless, stay current with your organization's longer-term aspirations and translate those to your career. Factor them in as you work through your Transition stage.

87—Age Does Matter

They say it doesn't matter, but it does. Step back and think about what the real ramifications are if there are too many "older" people in your company or organization. A case can be made that institutional and professional knowledge should be protected and valued. If there are too many transitions in the organization, the brain trust of the company could be compromised. This is common in companies where project and client experience are two critical factors to success. Career succession planning should be one of a company's highest priorities.

On the other hand, an organization cannot be successful without building the next generation of technologists and account managers. One of the biggest challenges for aging employees is the ability to relate to and reflect on the changing customer. Your clients will become more diverse and younger as you advance your career. Being able to understand and respond to a new generation of clients can be difficult but necessary. Look around you: what is the average age of your collegium, of your leadership? If you are considering the transition to retirement, or a late career reinvention, you may be one of the oldest. Don't resent that fact. Embrace it and think about what's next for you.

88—Working for "The Man" (or "The Woman")

I don't mean this in a critical way, but over time—especially at the Transition stage—you will begin to judge the value of your current work to society, your community, and your future life. You may have worked for someone, some

You may find yourself tired of working for an organization that's no longer aligned with your personal goals.

organization, for many years. Although the organization may have treated you fairly, unless you are an owner or part of executive management, you likely have not seen the upside of that growth in terms of equity. It may be time to evaluate whether you want to now direct your energy more toward yourself, your family, or your life goals.

I have been on executive teams working for The Man. And I have been a lower-level employee working for The Man, enthusiastically agreeing to help satisfy the organization's targets. Most recently, while an executive, I realized I no longer aspired to be a corporate leader. I wanted to create something on my own...something that would allow me to be my own boss. Something I could operate with pride.

Don't be afraid to weigh your feelings about your current work against what could be your future.

89—Leave as Friends

If you retire, you will leave your organization or company. If you reinvent your career, you may be able to do so within your current organization, but most likely you will simply leave. As you know, there is an art to leaving. Like leaving a neighborhood gathering or a family reunion, be aware that after you leave, people will talk about you. If you have worked hard during your career to leave positive impressions, why not depart in the same way? Spend time saying goodbye to your colleagues, and don't forget to thank the host. Your organization or company deserves the best from you.

Remember, too, that your decisions at work have influenced others. Some colleagues think you're great but others, perhaps, think not. The challenge is to identify those with whom you'd like to stay in touch, then make a commitment to do so. These relationships can be purely social, or they may help you as you reinvent yourself. You have built a lot of social capital with your colleagues. Find a way to unlock it as you transition to your new career.

90—Carry the Ball Over the Finish Line

You have decided to transition. You have set a date, your finances are in order, and you have an after-career plan. But you may have to wait for the best time to make the move. It may be at the end of the year, or after your bonus payout, or when you can secure health insurance. Emotionally you've made your decision and you're wrapping things up, at least in your own head. For some though, this may be a danger zone—you're ready to go but not fully engaged.

Instead, it's best to finish strong and with momentum. Remember King of the Hill? Leave at the top with your best year. Leave behind your best team—a better organization. You'll feel good departing after meeting your goals, both personally and organizationally. Don't forget a succession plan. You know your role and assignments best. Develop a plan for your managers that allows them to replace you without dropping the ball.

> *Don't let yourself get to a point where you are ineffective or are affecting others' attitudes or performance.*

91—Mental Acuity

My wife and I tease each other about our mental acuity. We are always ready to comment on the other's forgetfulness or ability to understand our young adult children. If you have lost your car keys in your pocket, or misplaced your cell phone in your favorite chair, or forgot to pay your utility bill, know this is normal. If you are asking your children to help with your devices or hear new words you don't understand, that even can be fun—at home. At work, though, these things can become a distraction and can impact your effectiveness.

I am not an expert on how the brain works. Therefore, I do not have any clinical recommendations. But I do believe there are things you can do to stay relevant. Changing your work routines may help. Immersing yourself in new environments can boost your effectiveness and help you stay in tune with your younger colleagues.

As you mature in your career, you should become better at focusing on what's most important in getting the job done. Organize your work and your calendar to eliminate distractions. At the same time, though, change things up. Work from a coffee shop, or use public transportation to get to the office. Have open discussions with your newer staff and colleagues. Be sure to embrace new technology; don't avoid it. Use it to your advantage. Always—always—be wary of the status quo.

92—"They Should Retire"

Sometimes your colleagues know when you should transition. Of course, they don't know your personal circumstances, but they see you at work and judge your performance every day. If you are a leader or manager, you are under the microscope more so than others. Are you present in meetings, can you problem-solve, are you in touch with the customers and employees? Are you respected by your peers and your organization?

We have all been in situations when a colleague has suggested that Janet or Joe "should have retired already." If you were Janet or Joe and had heard this, how would you feel?

If you take the time to honestly review your accomplishments and behaviors, you will know your effectiveness. So, while you're in your Transition stage, be sure to judge yourself more critically than ever before. Be truthful with yourself; be your toughest critic. Are you doing the job well? Are you keeping up? Are you still leading?

93—Because I Can

At points in your career, you can be pragmatic.

Whether you are thinking of retiring or reinventing yourself, go ahead, give it a try. Certainly, I am not suggesting you carelessly make decisions or move forward recklessly, but this is a time to do what you want to do, not what you have to do.

A friend of mine spent most of her career in firms seeking to lead, own, or strategically develop new businesses. After a successful career in the engineering industry being an "intrapreneur," she realized that her career aspiration had not been satisfied. She left a six-figure income, with full benefits, and an industry she had worked in for 30 years in order to buy her own company and become owner and CEO. She was able to use her professional network and teamed up with a colleague to purchase a struggling business and become the entrepreneur she had always wanted to be.

This may be an ideal time to be focused on yourself, your family, and your friends.

Maybe you choose to retire because you can. Having reached your career aspirations or having the assets to retire comfortably are good reasons in themselves to turn in the company computer, cell phone, and credit card. Your reasons to retire or reinvent can be very simple. If there's that clarity, you will be successful in your choice.

94—Always Wanted To

The motivation to Transition could be very straightforward. By this point, you have worked hard and have established some key mile markers along the way to help you pause and consider what's next. Many of my colleagues have their "number." Sometimes it's their age, sometimes it's the amount of time—hours in a day—that they want to spend with family and friends. Sometimes it's a financial number. Sometimes the decision is simply because they always wanted to "make the break."

Consider your career. You have worked five or six days a week, for 35 or 40 years. Consider the number of birthdays, soccer games, and holidays you have missed with your family and friends. I don't recommend you do the math on the number of days or hours you have dedicated to your career. It'll shock you ... perhaps even depress you. If you do that math though, you will realize you have given enough.

> *Your career may have consumed you over the years; now you can reward yourself for a career well-lived.*

It is time to reward yourself with retirement or reinvention. You have always wanted to take a three-month holiday, to be readily available for your first granddaughter, to *not* have a schedule.

95—A Suppressed E

You may have a strong interest to reinvent yourself. You have given away a lot of yourself over the years—not just your time and energy, but your creative and entrepreneurial spirit. Now, perhaps, you have the chance to start a small business with a friend or colleague. Maybe you have grander aspirations and want to start your own company, grow it, and capture equity from your entrepreneurial spirit.

A personal or professional reinvention is not easy. You have been working for someone, funded by someone, and been able to depend on colleagues and team members for years. Reinventing yourself is all "on you." You have to recommit yourself to new goals and new challenges. Depending on your path forward, you may work harder and longer hours to achieve your expectations than you did in your career.

The bottom line: if you choose to reinvent, do it for the right reasons. Having a great idea is not enough. You will only be successful if you are able to harness your passion, again. Critically evaluate your reinvention motivations.

Be absolutely convinced you have a strong passion—one that can only be satisfied by your new journey.

96—Life Is Too Short

As you approach the Transition stage, you will realize you have been working more years than not. So, don't wait too long to be a bit selfish. Be sure you have the time to spend in retirement or your new career. You will be "working" for yourself moving forward, but do it while you still can! Health, family, or financial issues may prevent you from enjoying these later years if you're not careful with your planning.

In all of my conversations with colleagues and friends, to a person, all say they have never regretted their decision to retire. In fact, most respond by saying, "should have retired years before." If retirement is not your thing, follow your heart. However, if you are looking to retire, the sooner the better.

97—Leaving It All Behind

Maybe one of the hardest shifts in your Transition stage is to "move on." Just like you may have gotten stuck during your career development, you can also get stuck in your Transition stage. The space between now and your next destination can be tight—or infinitely wide.

Of course, you should be proud of your accomplishments. But don't let them hold up your retirement or reinvention. Sure, it takes mental and emotional time to "release" yourself from your previous career aspirations. In retirement, you will no longer be CEO, director of operations or lead technical expert. You will become Jessica, Jim, or Colleen. No title, no business card, just you. But that's OK. You'll do just fine. The sooner you realize a new journey has begun, the sooner your journey can begin.

98—Who Am I Now?

The process of redefining yourself in retirement or reinvention—similar to the process you used to define your professional brand—may be difficult.

During your career, you likely evolved your personality and your behaviors to do well at the job. As you moved through your career, you probably became more opinionated, more self-assured, more decisive, and less patient. These skills were useful.

However, you may need new skills to navigate your retirement or reinvention.

Reconnecting with your family and close friends, and meeting new friends, will help. Hopefully, you are also eager to engage in new social networks.

The key: be open-minded, be prepared for change, and don't depend on just your past career skills to support you in the future.

99—Give Back

Giving back during and after a successful career is one way of thanking those who have helped you along the way. While you are pursuing your career it can be difficult to make the time necessary to fulfill all your obligations as a partner, leader, friend, or sibling. Carving out the time to volunteer, mentor, or support those who can benefit from your help is challenging. If you can find the time, you will certainly receive more than you give.

If you look hard enough, there are many ways you can give back to your communities, your public schools, or your industry. During a very busy period in my life when I was CEO, I also taught a university class in hydrogeology and coached my son's soccer team. I was also elected to be one of our township's supervisors. It was hectic and I am not sure how well I did with any of it. I learned that giving back takes commitment, but as it aligns with your passions, it will be well worth the effort. On the other hand, if you are not committed or passionate about your contributions, it is best to stay out of the game.

Find those contributions that are aligned with your passion!

As you approach the Transition stage of your career life cycle, it is wise to think about how you will spend your newfound time. Will it be to open a donut shop, live on a Caribbean island, or actively get involved in your community? Your decision will likely be a combination of spending time with family, friends, and your hobbies. But remember, you have knowledge that has been gained through years of experience, both in your career and in your life. Why not find a way to share yourself with others?

Share yourself with others and make a lasting impact on the future.

Giving back can take many forms. Find a way to share yourself with others and make a lasting impact on the future.

100—Financial Flexibility

I hope by now you have created the financial flexibility to choose your new path. Building wealth throughout your career may seem greedy or too unimportant at times. However, you will need that security to enjoy your post-career days.

If you choose to reinvent yourself, it will likely cost you additional money and energy—likely more than just continuing your existing career. And while some of us have dreamed of retiring rich and early, most of us know it's more complicated than that. "I just want to be healthy and have the assets to support myself and my family."

Remember—only a few of you reading this book will have an employee defined pension, and for most of you, Social Security will not be sufficient to support your intended way of life. Saving and investing are keys to a flexible future.

I had been thinking of retirement since I was in my forties. At that time, I picked an age to retire. But when I reached that age, I changed my mind, primarily because I was happy with my career and future opportunities. I only began my post-retirement financial planning five years ago. But I had been saving and investing along the way. Today, I have a great financial planner—someone I trust and who is aligned with my post-career ambitions.

You will find that securing this financial foundation is critical to being confident in your post-career plan.

SUMMARY

Transition is the fifth stage, and it's when you move out of your career to retire or perhaps create a new career. The most challenging part of this phase is the "when." When do you begin winding down your career or take the chance to reinvent yourself? When do you choose to leave the workforce? Should you have a retirement or startup party? A significant controlling factor is having the financial flexibility to choose your path forward.

This stage can be very exciting, but it usually takes time to transition. Some may want to do it quickly and leave it all behind, but typically it takes planning to successfully retire or plot a new career.

Whatever you decide, do it on your terms. Be thoughtful and proactive about your next steps, and develop a personal plan to achieve your desired outcomes.

Whatever you decide, do it on your OWN TERMS.

Afterword

The workplace is continuously changing, and you are in the middle, looking ahead and crafting your career. It is an exciting time to think about how we will work in the future. Current trends would lead us to believe that remote officing, virtual teams, and flexible assignments will continue to lead the way to a new workplace.

The employment models of today will need to change to attract and retain future employees. In the past, companies could create an alliance with an employee by offering security and a range of benefits for the employee and their family. Gradually, companies have been changing their "psychological contracts" with their employees toward providing a job within the context of their short-term business objectives. Long-term employment security is a way of the past, and the employee can't rely on securing a job for a lifetime. That makes career development and planning all the more important.

In addition to developing your career, you are also responsible for living the life you desire. Balancing your career and life aspirations is always a challenge, but I believe it is possible to have a successful career and a happy life. The perspective I urge you to take is to look at your career as a partner in supporting the life you desire.

In 2025, I will be releasing a new book titled A *Career and You Deserve—A Career Working for You!* This book is built to help career developers "balance" their career with their life. This book will describe a Career Life Partner Model, provide a Career Life Care Assessment, and coach you through the development of a Career Life Plan. I hope you have enjoyed *Own Your Career—No One Else Will* and will be interested in digging a bit deeper in my next book and learn how you can partner with your career to live the life you deserve.

Acknowledgments

Thanking everyone who has helped me in my career would be impossible. One of my biggest lessons has been, "you cannot have a successful career without a lot of help along the way!"

I start with a big thank you to my mother, Jane DeMaso-Goudreault, a first-generation immigrant from Italy, who was passionate about education and gave me great self-esteem. She had a successful career herself, fighting all the odds in a "man's world." I also admire and thank my sister, Yvonne Caamal Canul, who demonstrated to me how a life passion can lead to a successful career. Thank you, too, to my dad, Fernand Goudreault, for sharing his spirit of travel and adventure.

Many coworkers have supported and "put up with me" over the years. I want to thank Carol Anne Heart, Bob Karls, and Jerry Rick for believing in me and guiding my early career journey. Also, a thank you to my career colleagues Rosanna Ouellette, Gretchen Koehn, J.R. Toren, Raimond Baumans, Ann Massey, Joseph Sczurko, Les Panek, Bob Salazar, Bill MacDonald, and Brian Ricketts. All of you have pushed me when I needed it and pulled me up to see the bigger picture.

Several personal mentors have helped me balance my career with my life. Many thanks to Steve Vanderboom, Steve Schroeder, Mike Henley, Randi Yoder, Mike Enright, Russ Larimer, Olaf Pfannkuch, Herb Wright, and Alex Linderman.

A special thank you to those who encouraged me to add more Tidbits and complete this second edition to *Own Your Career—No One Else Will*. Thank you to Tina Raap, Monet Goudreault, Katlin Yoder Henley, Thomas Howe, Eric Bergsma, and Karen Helfrich.

About the Author

Paul Goudreault has over 40 years of experience as an executive leader in numerous roles, including founder and CEO of two multinational environmental consulting firms, as well as owner and CEO of a construction-manufacturing company. He is the founding partner of Enorine Partners, a leadership, business, and career coaching consultancy. Goudreault focuses on mentoring a new generation of leaders, developing and executing on organizational strategies, and employee career development.

Goudreault entered the workforce as a young geologist and created a successful career in the engineering and consulting industry. He has worked globally in more than thirty countries and has logged more than one hundred trips around the world. He has designed and implemented organizational transformations, including purchasing and integrating acquired companies, aligning organizations with their strategic intent, and designing and leading account-management programs. During his career, Goudreault has been responsible for $2 billion in sales from a portfolio of multinational clients. He has served on several not-for-profit boards supporting environmental stewardship.

He has been happily married for forty years to his wife Katie and has two children, Monet and Adrien. Stay in touch with the author at www.PaulGoudreault.com or Paul.Goudreault@EnorinePartners.com.